I0781884

Voices in Motion: Stories of Migration

RICARDO GÓMEZ

These stories are composites, drawn from interviews with dozens of migrants over the past decade. I changed names, combined experiences, fictionalized scenes. The people are invented. The experiences are real.

Table of Contents

Cast of Characters		iii
Introduction		v
1.	Luis	viii
2.	Carlos and Abdullah	11
3.	Miguel Angel	21
4.	Lucía	29
5.	Isabella	39
6.	José	49
7.	Gabriela and Cecilia	59
8.	Maria Cristina	71
9.	Francisco	81
10.	Elena	87
11.	Rosa	99
12.	Karina	107
13.	Javier	117
14.	Rodrigo	125
15.	Alejandro	135
Epilogue		143
Acknowledgments		145

Cast of Characters

These composite characters are drawn from interviews with dozens of migrants. They represent the diversity of Latino experiences in the United States.

Alejandro Ramirez — Mexican. Fled cartel violence in Michoacán, now runs a migrant resource center in Texas.

Carlos Gutierrez — Peruvian. Made a dangerous journey through Central America, befriended an Afghan refugee along the way.

Elena Torres — Venezuelan. Brought her children to Maryland, left her husband behind.

Francisco Herrera — Chilean. Immigration lawyer in Los Angeles. Fled Pinochet's regime as a young man.

Gabriela Torres — Mexican American (DACA). Daughter of Yakima Valley farmworkers, first in her family to graduate college.

Isabella Rodriguez — Uruguayan. Documentary filmmaker in New York. Won the green card lottery.

Javier Morales — Mexican. Undocumented meatpacking worker. Died in ICE detention after a workplace injury.

José Martínez — Colombian. Gay software engineer navigating Silicon Valley's diversity politics.

Karina Rivas — Panamanian. Survivor of trafficking and domestic violence. Now an advocate.

Lucía Gonzalez — Honduran. Former au pair, now a suburban mother in Maryland, navigating two identities.

Luis Ortega — Ecuadorian. Night janitor. Found community at Casa Latina in Seattle.

Maria Cristina Lopez — Spanish. Professor who mentors Latino students, confronting her own complicated position.

Miguel Angel Cruz — Cuban. Crossed on a raft. Mechanic and community leader in New Jersey.

Rodrigo Menjivar — Salvadoran. Deported after twenty years in the U.S. Murdered by gangs three months later.

Rosa Alvarez — Mexican. Mother of three U.S. citizen children. Separated by the ten-year bar after visiting her dying mother.

Introduction

The first person I interviewed for this book wouldn't look at me.

We were in a church basement in Los Angeles, metal folding chairs, a water-stained drop ceiling. She kept her eyes on her hands while she talked—about crossing the desert, about the coyote who abandoned them, about finding her brother's body three days later. She spoke in a flat, steady voice, like she was reading a grocery list. When she finished, she finally looked up.

"Why does it matter?" she asked. "Who's going to read this?"

I didn't have a good answer. I'm still not sure I do.

Over the past decade, I've sat across from dozens of people like her—in community centers and church basements, in living rooms and taco shops, in shelters and detention facilities. Day laborers and software engineers. Farmworkers and professors. People who crossed on rafts and people who flew in on student visas. Some had been in the country for thirty years. Others had arrived the week before.

What they had in common was that they'd agreed to tell me their stories.

I'm a researcher. I came to these conversations with questions about migration patterns and integration challenges, about identity formation and community resilience. I'd read the literature. I knew the statistics. What I wasn't prepared for was the weight of it—the accumulation of so many lives, so much loss, so much stubborn hope.

The numbers tell one story. Eleven million undocumented immigrants in the United States. Seven hundred thousand DACA recipients. Thousands of deaths in the desert every year. Detention facilities at capacity. Deportation flights leaving daily.

But numbers don't capture the father who works two jobs so his daughter can go to college, then watches her grow embarrassed by his accent. They don't capture the lawyer who fled a dictatorship, now fighting deportation cases he knows he'll lose. They don't capture the woman separated from her American children by a policy designed to punish her for visiting her dying mother.

This book is an attempt to hold both—the patterns and the particulars, the data and the lives it represents.

The fifteen characters in these pages are composites. I changed names, combined experiences, invented scenes. A woman I met in Seattle might appear in a story set in Texas. Two interviews conducted years apart might be woven into a single conversation. This is fictionalization—a way of telling truth through invention.

Some readers will be skeptical of this approach. If the stories aren't factually accurate, how can they be trusted?

Here's what I can tell you: Every fear in this book is real. Every hope. Every moment of resilience. The details have been rearranged, but the emotional core remains intact. When a character describes the terror of hearing a knock on the door, that terror was described to me, in those words, by someone who lived it. When a character talks about the loneliness of success—of making it, and still feeling like you don't belong—that's not something I imagined. Someone told me that. Many people told me that.

I fictionalized these stories to protect the people who shared them with me. I also fictionalized them because I believe fiction can sometimes reach places that journalism cannot. A composite character can carry the weight of many lives. A fictionalized scene can capture an emotional truth that a transcript might miss.

Whether I've succeeded is for you to judge.

The people in this book come from Mexico and Cuba, from Honduras and Venezuela, from Colombia and Uruguay and El Salvador and Peru. They work as janitors and filmmakers, as lawyers and farmworkers, as tech executives and trafficking survivors. Some have green cards. Some have DACA. Some have nothing—no papers, no protection, just the fact of their presence.

What unites them is simpler than any category: they left one life and tried to build another. That's the oldest human story there is.

I've organized these stories alphabetically by character name, not by theme or chronology. There's no arc here, no building argument. Just fifteen people, each with a story worth telling. Read them in order or skip around. Start with whoever catches your eye.

A few will make you angry. The systems that shape these lives—immigration courts, detention centers, border enforcement—are often cruel in ways that feel almost designed. A mother can be barred from her citizen children for a decade because she left the country to say goodbye to her dying mother. A worker can die in solitary confinement because he reported a safety violation. These are not aberrations. They are policy.

Other stories are quieter. A filmmaker trying to make something meaningful. A professor navigating her own complicated position. A man who finds dignity in work the world considers beneath notice.

I don't know what you'll take from these pages. I don't know if they'll change anything—any policy, any mind. But I believe they deserve to be read. I believe the people who trusted me with their experiences deserve to have those experiences witnessed, even in fictionalized form.

The woman in the church basement asked who would read this.

I hope it's you. I hope it matters.

1. Luis

The office building emptied at 5:47 every evening, give or take. Luis Ortega knew the rhythm—the rush of footsteps, the elevator chimes, the way conversations stopped mid-sentence as people grabbed their bags and pushed toward the doors. He'd wheel his cleaning cart out of the supply closet at 5:52, just as the last of them were pulling on their coats.

No one looked at him. That was fine.

Luis moved through the halls with his own kind of purpose, emptying trash cans, wiping down the conference tables, making his way floor to floor as the building settled into silence. He took pride in the work—not the work itself, exactly, but in the small things he could do within it.

The assistant on the fourth floor, the one who stayed late every night and always looked like she was about to cry—Luis had started leaving paper cranes on her desk. He'd learned to fold them from a YouTube video, practicing on napkins and receipt paper until he could make one in under two minutes. Red ones, blue ones, white ones from the copy room. She never said anything, probably didn't know where they came from. But they kept disappearing, which meant she was keeping them. That was enough.

On the executive floor, there was a man whose family photos were always crooked—knocked sideways by the careless swing of a briefcase or a jacket tossed over the chair. Every night, Luis straightened them. The wife and two kids in front of a Christmas tree. The whole family at what looked like a graduation. A trip to somewhere with palm trees. The man probably never noticed. But the photos were always level in the morning.

These were Luis's ways of existing in a world that preferred not to see him.

I first met Luis several years earlier, during a research project at Casa Latina, a nonprofit serving Seattle's immigrant community. When I reached out again for this book, he agreed to meet me after his shift.

He arrived still in his work uniform, a polo shirt with a faded logo. His accent reminded me of my grandmother, who had grown up in Quito.

"I came here ten years ago," he said, after we'd found a quiet corner. "I had nothing but a suitcase and a dream." He caught himself, smiled a little. "That's what people say, right? But it was true. It was exactly like that."

He talked about growing up in Quito. His father did construction when there was construction to do. His mother cleaned houses, took in laundry, sold *empanadas de viento* from a cart near the Parque El Ejido on weekends—whatever put food on the table.

"Five kids," Luis said. "I was the oldest, so I helped. After school, I'd shine shoes downtown, sell newspapers. I got good at spotting the tourists—they'd give you a few extra sucres if you smiled right."

He was quiet for a moment, zipping and unzipping his jacket.

"I liked school. But it's hard to pay attention when you're hungry, you know? I finished high school. Barely. But university?" He shook his head. "No."

His uncle Pedro had gone to the States years before. When Pedro came back to visit and saw how things were, he helped Luis get a tourist visa.

"The day after I turned eighteen, I was on a plane. Cheapest ticket there was." Luis paused. "I hugged my mom at the airport. Told her I'd be back in a month."

He looked at me. "We both knew."

Pedro picked him up in Atlanta. They drove to a small apartment in Doraville—a neighborhood full of other Latinos, Mexicans and Guatemalans mostly. That first night, they sat on the balcony with cheap beer and watched the city lights.

"My uncle got me a job washing dishes where he worked. But after a month, my visa expired." Luis looked down at his hands. "And then I was something else. *Indocumentado.*"

He described the fear. How it gets into your body. Every siren, every uniform, every knock on the door.

"You know that movie, *Paraíso Travel?*" he asked. "There's a guy who finally makes it to New York with his girlfriend. He goes out for a cigarette, sees a cop, and just—runs. Keeps running until he's lost. Can't find his way back to her."

Luis shook his head slowly. "I didn't have a girlfriend. Just my uncle. But I understood that guy. That panic. There were nights I planned escape routes in my head. Just in case."

He couldn't run. He couldn't go back. So he worked.

Construction when he could find it. Mowing lawns. A week cleaning up after a tornado in Alabama—eighteen hours a day, cash at the end of each shift.

"Some people cheated me. There was this job framing houses. Two weeks, no days off. When I asked for my money, the foreman laughed. Said he'd call immigration if I didn't leave." Luis opened his hands. "So I left. What else could I do?"

After six months, things went bad with his uncle. Pedro lost his job. Started drinking. The apartment got smaller.

One morning Luis put his things in a bag and took a Greyhound to Miami.

"Miami was different. The heat, the ocean, all those palm trees. For a while I thought: okay, this is a new start." He smiled. "I got a job in a Cuban restaurant. Learned to make *cafecito* the right way—strong, sweet, in those little cups. But the humidity. *Dios mío.* Worse than Quito in January."

He moved again. Orlando—he worked at one of the big theme parks, pushing a broom, invisible in the crowd. Charlotte—he learned carpentry from a contractor who didn't ask questions. New Orleans—he spent months helping rebuild houses after Katrina.

"That was hard," he said. "But good, too. Like I was doing something real."

Every city was the same pattern: find work, find somewhere to sleep, keep your head down. But sometimes there were surprises.

"In Charlotte, this old man caught me sleeping in his tool shed. Mr. Johnson. White guy, maybe seventy. I thought: this is it, he's calling the police." Luis paused. "Instead he asked if I was hungry. Gave me a job. Let me sleep on his couch for three months."

"In New Orleans, there was a priest. Father Miguel. He had this little church that helped immigrants. Didn't matter if you had papers or not. He used to say, 'We're all God's children.' He meant it, too."

Luis was quiet for a moment.

"For every person like that, there were ten more ready to cheat you. And the fear never stopped. Ten years, and it never stops."

He came to Seattle three years after leaving Ecuador. He'd heard there was work.

"I found this company. Nightshine Cleaning, something like that. They hired a lot of immigrants. I thought I'd gotten lucky."

They told him they'd hold his first two weeks' pay as a deposit. In case he broke something. He was desperate. He said okay.

Two weeks passed. Three. Every time he asked about his money, there was a reason. The check was coming. The owner was traveling. The paperwork was delayed.

"A month in, I was cleaning a big office building downtown. Still hadn't seen one dollar. Then the supervisor came and said they were letting me go. 'Downsizing.' Just like that—no job, no wages, nothing."

Luis tried to argue. Said he'd report them.

"They told me: 'Go ahead. We'll call ICE.'"

He spread his hands. "So I left."

He was homeless after that. Sleeping in parks, under the freeway, sometimes at a shelter when there was room. Going two, three days without food.

"I felt like nothing," he said quietly. "Like I wasn't even a person anymore."

One afternoon he went to the public library. Not to read. It was warm, and they had bathrooms.

"I looked bad. Dirty clothes, hadn't showered in a week. Most people looked right through me. But this librarian—Maria—she came up and asked if I needed help. If I was hungry."

Maria, it turned out, specialized in helping immigrants. She knew the system—which agencies to call, which shelters had beds, where to get legal help.

"She bought me a sandwich from the café downstairs. And she listened. Then she started making calls, pulling out pamphlets. She told me about Casa Latina."

He paused.

"It wasn't just the information. She looked at me like I was a person. Like I mattered."

He left the library that day with food in his stomach and, for the first time in months, something like a plan.

Casa Latina changed everything.

Luis showed me a workbook he carried in his backpack—English exercises, pages worn soft from use. The organization had classes in language, computers, workers' rights. They'd connected him with a lawyer who was helping him recover the wages Nightshine had stolen.

"But it's not just that," he said. "It's having people. I'm not alone anymore."

He pointed around the room. A man named Javier was teaching him Excel. A woman named Maria—different Maria—was helping him practice for job interviews. For a month now, he'd had steady work through their dispatch program. Fair wages. Safe conditions. A paycheck he could count on.

"There were times I almost gave up," Luis said. "Almost went back to Ecuador. The loneliness, the fear—it wears on you."

He shook his head.

"But I've come too far."

As evening came, we walked toward downtown. The sky was going orange over the Olympics.

Luis slowed when we reached City Hall. The building was all glass and steel, lit from inside, the plaza in front of it nearly empty.

"I walk past here a lot," he said. "It always feels far away, you know? Like a place where people make decisions about my life, but I'm not allowed inside. No voice. No vote. Nothing."

He stood there for a moment. Then he smiled—a strange, crooked smile.

"But here's the thing. I've slept in there."

He pointed to the main entrance, the heavy glass doors.

"A few years ago, bad winter. Really cold. The city opened it up as a shelter. I slept there for a week. A cot in one of the meeting rooms. Marble floors, tall ceilings, portraits of all the mayors looking down at us."

He laughed softly.

"Can you imagine? Me. *Indocumentado.* Sleeping in City Hall. Right in the middle of everything." He shook his head. "Sometimes I still can't believe it."

We stood there a moment longer, the building glowing above us.

We kept walking. Luis pointed to Pioneer Square, where he used to sleep on benches. Where strangers sometimes bought him coffee. He said he used to feel ashamed, walking through here. Now he sees it differently.

"It reminds me I survived."

Near the waterfront, the conversation turned to the future. I could hear something shift in his voice—a weight he'd been carrying the whole time.

"I think about going back," he said. "Just to visit. To see my mom. My brothers and sisters have kids now—I've only seen them in pictures." He was quiet. "I want to show them it meant something. All of this."

But if he left, he couldn't come back. That was the reality. Everything he'd built would be gone.

"Last year my cousin called. My grandmother was dying." His voice caught. "I wanted to go. I wanted to say goodbye. But I couldn't."

He looked out at the water.

"I said goodbye on the phone. Bad connection. Kept cutting out."

We walked in silence for a while.

"That's the price," Luis said finally. "You're never all the way here. You can never go back. You live in between."

We circled back to Casa Latina. The streetlights were on. Through the windows, I could see people in the English class, heads bent over worksheets. Phones ringing at the front desk.

Luis stopped at the entrance.

"Most people don't see us," he said. "We clean their offices, mow their lawns, cook their food. We're out of sight."

He looked through the glass at the people inside—the ones taking classes, the ones answering phones, the ones just sitting and talking, glad to have somewhere to be.

"But here," he said, "we're not invisible."

He pulled a folded square of paper from his jacket pocket—a paper crane, white, slightly crumpled. He turned it over in his fingers.

"*Aquí existimos*," he said quietly.

Then he pushed open the door and went inside.

2. Carlos and Abdullah

The bell above the door jingled as I stepped into the deli, drawn by the smell of fresh bread. Behind the counter, two men in crisp aprons were arranging pastries in the display case. One looked up and smiled.

"*Hola, bienvenido*," he said. "What can I get for you?"

"Still deciding. Are you new here?"

He nodded. "First day. I'm Carlos. This is Abdullah."

The other man gave a small wave. There was an ease between them—the kind that comes from knowing someone beyond words—despite what seemed like very different backgrounds.

The owner, Sarah, came over. "I see you've met our newest team members. They've come a long way to be here."

Carlos glanced at Abdullah. "A very long way."

I noticed the calluses on their hands, a pale scar running up Abdullah's forearm. "How about you surprise me," I said. "Your favorite sandwich. I have a feeling it'll be good."

They turned to each other, a quick conversation passing in the tilt of a head, the quirk of an eyebrow. Then they got to work.

I came back the next day, and the day after. By the end of the week, they'd agreed to tell me their story.

We sat at a corner table after the lunch rush. Carlos did most of the talking at first—his English was rougher than Abdullah's, but he had more to say, or maybe a greater need to say it.

He'd grown up in Villa El Salvador, a sprawl of cinderblock houses on the sandy outskirts of Lima. His parents worked at a textile factory in the industrial zone. He was the oldest of three.

"I was always in trouble," Carlos said. "Not bad trouble. *Político.*" He smiled slightly. "At San Marcos, I organized protests. Land rights for the *campesinos*, labor rights in the factories. The professors encouraged me. Other people—" He shrugged. "Not so much."

The threats started his second year. Phone calls where no one spoke. Notes slipped under his door: *Cállate o muere.* Shut up or die.

Then, one night walking home through Miraflores, a group of men pulled him into an alley. They worked him over with pipes and boots. Cracked two ribs, broke his nose, left him in the gutter.

"They said it was a warning. They said next time they would make me disappear. *Desaparecido.*" He let the word hang. In Peru, it carried the weight of history. "I believed them."

He left Lima two weeks later. A bus north to Ecuador, then Colombia. Then the jungle.

Abdullah had been listening, his tea untouched. When Carlos finished, he looked down at his hands—broad hands, scarred across the knuckles.

"For me, it was my father," he said.

He spoke carefully, precisely. His English had a formal quality—he'd learned it translating for American soldiers in Kabul, sitting in on meetings, repeating words until they became his own.

"My father was an elder in our village, in Logar province. He spoke against the Taliban. Not with weapons—with words. Everyone respected him." Abdullah paused. "One night, they came."

He didn't describe it in detail. He didn't need to. They dragged his father into the street. They made the family watch.

"After that, my brothers and I were marked. I had a permit for the evacuation—because of my work with the Americans, the SIV program. But when the day came—" He shook his head. "You saw the pictures. The airport. The crowds. Taliban at every checkpoint."

They'd recognized him. Told him he would die like his father.

He spent weeks in hiding, moving between safe houses in Kabul. Then Pakistan. Then Iran. He sold his wife's jewelry, his father's watch, everything. He paid smugglers. He flew to Brazil on a forged passport.

"Why South America?" I asked.

"*Chāra nadāshtam*," he said. Then, in English: "I had no choice. It was the only door open."

They met in the jungle.

The Darién Gap—sixty miles of rainforest between Colombia and Panama. No roads, no law, no way around. Migrants from everywhere funneled through: Venezuelans, Haitians, Cubans, Afghans, Bangladeshis, Chinese, Senegalese. Thousands every week, all moving north.

Carlos had been walking for two days when he noticed the Afghan struggling behind him. Alone, carrying a pack too heavy for his frame, stopping every hundred meters to catch his breath.

"He looked like he was going to fall down and not get up," Carlos said. "I didn't know anything about him. I just knew he needed help."

He offered to carry the pack. Abdullah hesitated—they had no common language beyond fragments of English and gestures—but eventually handed it over.

That night, they made camp near each other. Carlos shared his rice and canned fish. Abdullah shared his water purification tablets. They pointed at their chests.

"Car-los."

"Ab-dull-lah."

That was the beginning.

The jungle was worse than either had imagined.

"The mud," Carlos said. "You sink to your knees. Sometimes deeper. It smells like rot, like things dying. And it holds you—every step you have to pull yourself out."

The rivers were fast and brown with rain. They crossed on ropes strung between trees, the current tearing at their legs. Carlos saw a woman lose her grip. She went under and didn't come back up. No one could stop. No one could help.

"You just keep walking," he said quietly. "You have to."

At night, the darkness was total. Sounds came from everywhere—insects screaming, frogs, things crashing through the undergrowth. They slept in shifts, taking turns with a cheap flashlight. The beam only made the darkness beyond it worse.

The *Clan del Golfo* controlled the crossing. For a fee, they sold colored bracelets—yellow, green, red—that were supposed to mean safe passage. Carlos and Abdullah paid. They never knew if it mattered.

"How did you communicate?" I asked. "Those first days?"

They looked at each other and laughed—the first time I'd seen them laugh together.

"Hands," Carlos said, miming climbing, swimming, eating.

"Pictures," Abdullah said. "In the mud. I would draw a snake"—he sketched a wavy line in the air—"and point ahead. Danger."

"My English was nothing," Carlos said. "His was better. But we both knew some words. 'Water.' 'Sleep.' 'Stop.' The important ones."

"And when words failed—" Abdullah shrugged. "*Fahmīdīm.* We understood anyway."

On the fourth night, Abdullah got sick. Fever, chills, cramps that doubled him over. He couldn't keep water down.

"I told him to go," Abdullah said. "I told him I would slow him down. That I would die there and he should save himself."

Carlos shook his head. "I told him to shut up. In Spanish. Very bad words." He almost smiled. "I don't think he understood, but he got the idea."

For two days, Carlos half-carried him. He rigged a sling from a torn shirt and draped Abdullah's arm over his shoulders. They moved at a crawl. Other migrants passed them, some offering water, most just hurrying on.

On the second night, the fever broke. Abdullah woke up soaked in sweat, weak but lucid. Carlos was asleep beside him, still gripping his arm.

"That's when I knew," Abdullah said. He didn't finish the sentence. He didn't need to.

Three days later, Carlos's feet gave out—blisters gone septic, every step like walking on glass. Abdullah returned the favor. He took the packs, let Carlos lean on him, kept them both moving.

"We made a deal," Carlos said. "Not with words. Just—" He looked at Abdullah. "If one falls, the other picks him up. That's the deal."

They emerged from the jungle and kept moving north. Panama. Costa Rica. Nicaragua. Honduras. Guatemala. Mexico. Buses when they could pay. Walking when they couldn't. Hiding from police, from gangs, from men who saw migrants as prey.

At the U.S. border, they joined thousands of others camped in the dust outside Tijuana. Waiting.

There was an app—CBP One—that let asylum seekers schedule appointments. Every day, Carlos and Abdullah tried. Every day, they failed.

"The photo," Carlos said, his jaw tightening. "The app couldn't recognize our faces. We would take the picture, submit, error. Again, error. A hundred times."

"Other people had the same problem," Abdullah said. "People with dark skin. The app was made for—" He paused. "For other faces."

Eventually they got through. But there were never any appointments. They checked at dawn, at noon, at midnight. Days became weeks. Weeks became months.

"We made it a joke," Abdullah said. "The app gods. We would bow to the phone. Once we left our last chocolate bar in front of it. An offering." He smiled faintly. "The app gods were not pleased."

They volunteered at the camp to pass the time. Carlos taught Spanish to kids from Afghanistan and Haiti. Abdullah helped at the medical tent, his translator's instincts useful for patients who spoke no English or Spanish. At night, in their patched tent, they studied for the future they weren't sure would come.

"The waiting was the worst," Carlos said. "In the jungle, you're moving. At the border, you're just—" He opened his hands. "*Atrapado.* Trapped."

Then one day, it happened.

Abdullah was checking the app—the same ritual, the same low expectations—when he made a sound Carlos had never heard from him.

"I thought someone had died," Carlos said. "I came running."

Abdullah held up the phone. Two appointments. Same day. Back to back.

"A glitch," Abdullah said. "The system made a mistake. But I didn't care. I just kept looking at it, afraid it would disappear."

They presented themselves at the port of entry the next morning. The interviews took hours. They told their stories— the alley in Lima, the street in Logar—and showed their scars. At the end, they were given papers. Temporary status. They could stay while their cases were processed.

"How long?" Carlos had asked the officer.

"Years," the officer said. "Maybe."

It didn't matter. They were through.

They came to Portland because someone at the border had mentioned work. Sarah hired them within a week.

"She didn't know us," Carlos said. "She saw two guys who needed a chance. That was enough for her."

They rented an apartment together. Two mattresses, a hot plate, a table where they studied English and planned for what came next. Carlos enrolled in community college—political science, eventually. Abdullah was working with a lawyer to bring his wife and daughter from Pakistan.

"Fatima," he said, when I asked. "And Zara. She's four now. She was walking, just learning, when I left." He pulled out his phone and showed me a picture: a woman with tired, intelligent eyes, holding a girl in a bright dress. "Two years I haven't seen them. But we're close now. *Inshallah*."

A year later, I was back in Portland. I stopped by the deli.

They looked different. More settled. Carlos had put on weight—"*Las tortas de Sarah*," he said, patting his stomach. Abdullah was wearing a ring.

"Fatima and Zara?"

His face opened. "Three months. They came three months ago."

He didn't elaborate. He didn't need to.

We sat at the same corner table. Afternoon light came through the windows.

"Do you think about it?" I asked. "The crossing?"

Carlos was quiet for a moment. "Every day. There were people who didn't make it. People we walked with. You don't forget."

"But you also can't regret," Abdullah said. "You did what you had to do. You survived. That's not—" He searched for the word. "That's not something to be ashamed of."

I asked what the experience had taught them.

Carlos considered. "That borders are just lines. People are people."

"And that you can't do it alone," Abdullah said. "I would have died in that jungle. Carlos would have died. We kept each other alive." He paused. "That's not poetry. It's just what happened."

Carlos reached over and gripped Abdullah's shoulder. Abdullah put his hand over his. They stayed like that for a moment, not speaking.

Then the bell above the door jingled—a customer—and they stood, reaching for their aprons.

"*Vamos*," Carlos said.

They moved behind the counter, already in sync. One reached for the bread as the other reached for the meat. One stepped left as the other stepped right. No words, no hesitation. The kind of coordination that takes years to build, or a jungle.

I watched them work—two men from opposite ends of the world who'd found each other in the mud and carried each other out.

The customer took her sandwich. The bell jingled. The afternoon went on.

3. Miguel Angel

The smell of motor oil and roasting pork. Miguel Ángel
Cruz was bent over the engine of a 1957 Chevy Bel Air, his
hands black to the wrists with grease. Through the open garage
door, I could see the banners of the Cuban festival a block
away—red, white, blue, snapping in the breeze. Salsa drums
drifted in on the humid Union City air.

"*¡Coño, Miguel!*" A voice cut through the clatter of the shop.
"Still got your head buried in an engine while the rest of us are
out there living?"

Miguel straightened, wiping his hands on a rag tucked into
his belt. A heavyset man in a white guayabera was crossing the
garage floor.

"Raúl, *mi hermano.*" Miguel's voice was sandpaper and
warmth. "Someone has to keep these *cacharros* running so you
can impress the ladies."

"Anita's asking for you. Says you owe her a dance from last
year."

"Tell her I've been practicing." Miguel did a quick shuffle
on the oil-stained concrete, work boots scraping. "Give me one
hour."

Raúl left laughing. Miguel turned and noticed me in the
doorway.

"Ah—the professor. Carmela's friend, *¿verdad?*" He crossed
the shop and shook my hand, leaving a smear of grease on my
palm. "Forgive the mess. But come, I'll close up and we walk to

the festival together. You want my story? I'll tell you on the way."

We fell into step toward the music, the drums getting louder with each block.

"You want to understand how I got here," Miguel said. "First you have to understand what we were leaving."

He told me about the *período especial.* The Special Period. After the Soviet Union collapsed, Cuba lost everything—oil, machinery, food, money. The early nineties.

"When the Soviets fell, it was like someone pulled the plug on the whole island. The *bodegas* were empty. We stood in line for hours for our ration—a little rice, a few beans. Meat?" He made a sound, half-laugh, half-disgust. "*Olvídate.*"

They had a saying: "The three biggest failures of the Revolution were breakfast, lunch, and dinner."

"The blackouts were every day. *Apagones.* I did homework by candlelight more nights than not. My mother boiled banana peels to make soup—just to have something hot in our bellies. My father traded his skills in the black market. He'd fix someone's car, they'd give him a few eggs. A bit of pork if he was lucky."

Miguel's face darkened.

"The hardest part was watching my parents. They did everything right. Worked hard, believed in the system. And still we were hungry. Still we had nothing."

He told me about *fe.* "You know what that means? Faith. But in Cuba, *fe* meant something else—*familia en el extranjero.*

Family abroad. If you had cousins in Miami who could send dollars, you survived. A bar of soap, some aspirin—these were treasures. We had no one."

We'd reached the edge of the festival grounds. Families everywhere, the smell of garlic and sofrito, kids chasing each other between the stalls. Miguel stopped walking.

"That's when I decided. I had to go."

He tried three times to cross the Straits of Florida.

"First time, the raft broke apart before we cleared Cuban waters. Inner tubes splitting, ropes coming loose. We swam back to shore in the dark, trying not to drown."

Second time, they made it further—maybe twenty miles out. Then the U.S. Coast Guard appeared.

"*Pies mojados*, they called us. Wet feet. If they caught you in the water, they sent you back. Only if you touched dry land could you stay." He shook his head. "They put us on a cutter and delivered us to Havana like packages. I spent two weeks in a cell. When I got out, I started planning again."

The third attempt, they were careful. Five of them. They built the raft in a friend's garage, working only at night. Inner tubes from truck tires. Scrap lumber. A piece of sailcloth for shade.

"We launched at three in the morning. No moon—just stars and black water."

Miguel's voice dropped. He wasn't looking at me anymore. He was back on that raft.

"First day wasn't bad. We paddled, we rested, we watched the horizon. Cuba disappeared behind us. By afternoon, the sun was a hammer. We had jugs of water, but not enough. A few sips every couple hours. That's all we allowed ourselves."

At night, they saw lights—a ship, far off. They argued in whispers. What if it was the Coast Guard? They stayed dark and let it pass.

"Second day, one of the men—Tomás—started vomiting. Couldn't stop. Seasickness, the sun, dehydration—who knows. He couldn't keep water down. We thought he would die right there on the raft."

They drifted. The current was pulling them north, but slowly. They had no instruments, no way to know how far they'd come. The sea was endless in every direction.

"That night, the sharks found us."

He said it simply. But I saw his hands tighten on the rag.

"Fins. Circling. At first just one or two, then more. One of them bumped the bottom of the raft—I felt it through the tubes, this thud that went up my spine. We sat frozen. Nobody moved, nobody breathed. I could hear them in the water, that sound they make when they surface. *Fssshhh*. Like they're tasting the air."

How long?

"I don't know. Hours. It felt like the whole night. I remember thinking about my mother—how she would never know what happened to me. How she would wait and wait and I would just be gone. I thought about slipping into the water, letting it be over. But then I thought: no. The only way out is forward. Swim or drown."

Third day. They saw birds. Then a smudge on the horizon that might be land.

"We paddled with everything we had. Our hands were raw—blisters broken open, bleeding into the water. Tomás couldn't help; we just told him to hold on. The shore got closer. We could see buildings, palm trees, cars moving on a road."

A boat appeared—they couldn't tell if it was Coast Guard or fishermen.

"We paddled harder. My arms were on fire. Fifty feet from the beach. Forty. Thirty. The waves were pushing us in, but too slow, too slow. I saw the boat turning toward us."

He jumped out when the water reached his chest. He ran, fell, got up, kept going. The sand was white and hot under his hands.

"When I touched dry ground—" His voice cracked. "I fell on my face and kissed it. *Pies secos.* Dry feet. I had nothing. No money, no papers, no food. The clothes on my back, and those were soaked with salt. But I was free."

***

We stood at the edge of the festival. The music swirled around us, but Miguel was still far away.

"Come," he said finally. "Enough of that. Let me buy you some *ropa vieja,* and then I really do have to find Anita."

We got plates of shredded beef and found a bench. Between bites, I asked what came after the beach.

"I slept on that same beach for a week. Sand for a mattress, stars for a roof. *Muy romántico*, eh?" He laughed. "But romance doesn't fill the stomach."

He drifted to Miami, then north when he heard there was work in New Jersey—a Cuban community that needed mechanics. He walked into every shop he could find.

"My English was garbage. I'd point at an engine and say 'I fix.' That's all I knew. They looked at me like I was crazy."

Then he found Ernesto. A old *habanero* who ran a shop in Union City.

"He looked at me for a long time. I was skinny, dirty, desperate. He said, '*Asere*, you look like something the sea spit out. But if you fix cars like you look hungry, you got a job.'"

Ernesto taught him everything. American engines, customer service, how to build a life.

"There was an old man who came in with a Chevy. A '52, beautiful bones but falling apart. Everyone else had turned him away. But I looked at that car and—" Miguel paused. "I saw myself. Beaten down, yes. But not broken."

He worked on it for weeks. Nights, weekends. When he got it running, the old man wept.

"That's when I understood. I don't just fix cars. I fix people. I give them back something they thought was lost."

Over the years, Miguel's shop became a gathering place. Somewhere immigrants could find work, advice, or just someone who'd listen.

"It happened without me planning it. One day I'm changing oil. Next day I'm making *cafecito* for Doña Rosa while she tells me her grandson needs a job. Week after that, I'm translating for a family at the DMV."

The festival had started as a block party—Miguel and a few other Cuban business owners. Now it filled the streets every summer.

"I look around at all this—" He gestured at the crowd, the music, the Cuban flags everywhere. "And I think: this is why I crossed. Not just for me. To build something. A piece of home."

But the community wasn't always easy. There were old wounds, old arguments.

"You see that man?" Miguel nodded toward a well-dressed man holding court at a nearby table, voice booming. "Benito Fuentes. For him, everything is simple. You hate Castro or you're a traitor. No middle ground."

"And you?"

"I left for a reason. I'm not going back." Miguel's jaw tightened. "But I can't hate the island that made me. I can't pretend my family doesn't still live there."

He reached into his back pocket and pulled out a photograph, soft with age. A woman, two children, standing in front of a concrete house.

"My sister Elena. Her kids—my nephew and niece. I haven't seen them in twenty-three years."

I looked at the faded faces.

"She calls when she can. The connection is always terrible—delays, static. Her kids are grown now. Married. I've never met them." He looked at the photo a moment longer, then slid it carefully back into his wallet. "That pain doesn't go away, *chico*. You just learn to carry it."

The sun was dropping. The festival would go late, but Miguel had promised Anita.

We walked back to the shop. The Bel Air was waiting, hood still up.

"You know what I love about these old cars?" Miguel ran his hand along the fender, a gesture of tenderness. "They built them to last. To be repaired, again and again. Not like now, where everything is made to throw away."

He picked up a wrench, weighed it in his hand.

"People are like that too. We break down. Life beats us up. But we can be fixed. We can keep running." He nodded toward the festival lights coming on down the block. "Everyone here— we're proof. We made the crossing. We're still going."

He bent over the engine, then looked up with a grin.

"Now go enjoy the festival, professor. Eat more *ropa vieja*. Maybe find a girl to dance with." He winked. "And me—I have a date with Anita, and this old Chevy isn't going to fix herself."

The wrench rang against metal as I walked away. Behind me, salsa drums and the smell of roasting pork. Ahead, the evening crowd filling the streets.

I looked back once. Miguel was already lost in the engine, his hands working, bringing something broken back to life.

4. Lucía

The pancake batter sizzled. Lucía's phone was wedged between her ear and shoulder—loss prevention on the fundraiser budget, Barbara Whitman's objections, the silent politics of suburban motherhood—while she flipped pancakes with one hand and stopped her four-year-old from baptizing the table in syrup with the other.

"Mama, I want the Mickey one."

"One second, *mi amor*—yes, Barbara, I understand the concern, but if we adjust the venue costs—"

The syrup won. A golden river spread across the oak.

"*Ay*, Sofia—" Lucía grabbed the paper towels, phone clattering to the floor. "I'll call you back."

She mopped the syrup, plated the pancakes (neither Mickey-shaped—she'd never mastered shapes), and finally dropped into a chair with coffee that had gone cold half an hour ago. Daniel, seven, ate with silent concentration. Sofia kicked the table leg in a rhythm designed to fray nerves.

This was the life she'd built. Suburban Maryland, two kids, a four-bedroom house with a swing set in the backyard. Ten years and three thousand miles from San Pedro Sula.

She should feel grateful. She was grateful.

And yet.

"Tell me about home," I said.

We were in her living room after the school drop-off. Beige walls, family portraits in matching frames, a sectional sofa that looked like it had never been sat on.

Lucía tucked her feet beneath her. "San Pedro? What do you want to know—the postcards or the truth?"

"Whatever you want to tell me."

She was quiet for a moment. "My family was middle class. My father worked for a shipping company; my mother taught primary school. We had a house in Colonia Moderna—nice streets, mango trees, a neighbor who played accordion on Sunday mornings. When I was small, it felt safe."

She told me how that changed. The *maras* spreading through the city. Boys she'd grown up with disappearing into the gangs or into the ground. A classmate shot outside his house for wearing the wrong color.

"By the time I finished university, my parents were afraid to let me walk to the corner store." She looked at the window—the empty cul-de-sac, the lawns like green carpet. "They started talking about me leaving. My mother's cousin had done the au pair program, married an American. They thought: this is how Lucía gets out."

Her father drove her to the airport in San Pedro. She remembered the smell of diesel and fried plantains from the vendors outside. He didn't cry—he never cried—but his hands shook when he hugged her.

"He said, '*Mija*, you were always too big for this place. Go find where you fit.'" She smiled, but it didn't reach her eyes. "I think he meant it as a blessing. But sometimes it felt like he was telling me I didn't belong."

Baltimore, 2007. She stepped off the plane with a rolling suitcase and fifty words of English.

The au pair agency had matched her with the Harringtons—Michael, who did something with consulting, and Sarah, who'd left marketing to raise twin boys. Their house in Bethesda had more bathrooms than her family's home had rooms.

"The first month, I cried every night."

She said it simply, without self-pity.

"Not because they were unkind. Sarah was wonderful—patient, generous. She corrected my English without making me feel stupid. But I had a university degree. In Honduras, I was someone. Here, I was the girl who couldn't remember the word for 'dustpan.'"

She learned the rhythms of American suburban life. The minivan circuit—soccer, piano, Kumon. Birthday parties that cost more than her father earned in a month. The strange silence of big houses where everyone had their own room and the TV played to no one.

"Sarah used to ask about my life back home. I could tell she wanted to understand." Lucía paused. "But she'd complain about being 'stressed' because the landscapers came on the wrong day. And I'd think about my mother, who still walked three blocks to buy water because the pipes didn't work."

She started taking classes at the community college—partly curiosity, partly necessity. Her communications degree meant nothing here.

"I had the knowledge," she said, "but not the right piece of paper."

She met David at the Harringtons' Fourth of July barbecue. Flag bunting, Bud Light in coolers, children waving sparklers across the lawn.

"I was hiding in the kitchen. Everyone was outside watching fireworks, but I just—needed a minute. The noise, the crowd, all that aggressive happiness." She shook her head. "In Honduras we have fiestas too, but this felt different. Performed."

David found her at the sink, washing dishes that didn't need washing.

"He didn't ask why I was inside. He just picked up a towel and started drying."

He was Michael's college roommate. An engineer—quiet, methodical, the kind of person who seemed embarrassed by his own presence. They talked for two hours. He'd been to Guatemala once, a college service trip, and he asked her real questions. Not *Is it dangerous?* but *What do you miss?* Not *Do you like it here?* but *What's the hardest part?*

"I told him about Lago de Yojoa—this lake where my family went for Semana Santa. The way the water looked like gold at sunset. My grandmother's *tamales de elote*, wrapped in banana leaves." She smiled. "He listened like it mattered. Like I mattered."

The romance was slow. He was awkward about the power dynamic—she was still technically an employee in his friend's house. For months it was just coffee, walks, long emails.

"He asked my father's permission. Over Skype." She laughed. "My father, who could barely work the computer, sat there in his good shirt while this *gringo* stumbled through formal Spanish. Papá said yes. Then he called me and said, 'His Spanish is terrible, but I can see his heart.'"

They married two years later. Small ceremony—David's family, a few friends, no one from Honduras.

"The flights were too expensive. The visas too uncertain." She looked down at her ring—modest diamond, white gold. "I cried during the ceremony. Everyone thought they were happy tears."

She paused.

"They were. Mostly. But I kept thinking: my grandmother will never see this. Marcos can't walk me down the aisle. I'm becoming someone new, and I don't know who."

Marriage changed her legal status but not the feeling of displacement. She had a green card now, then citizenship. She could work, drive, vote. The low hum of fear that had followed her since her visa expired—it faded, mostly.

But the house David bought felt like a costume she was wearing.

"Four bedrooms. A two-car garage. A yard with a swing set." She gestured around the room. "The neighbors wave, and I wave back, and I think: *Do they see me? Or do they see David's wife? The house? The minivan?*"

She joined a book club. The women talked about memoirs and beach vacations and kitchen renovations. She sat with her wine and smiled and thought about her cousin back home, who'd been shot in a robbery last year. She thought about her mother, still boiling water because the pipes had never been fixed.

"I never say these things. I bring banana bread. I compliment their kitchens. I make my voice lighter, my accent softer."

She looked at me directly.

"David doesn't see it. He thinks I'm happy. And I am—I *am*—but sometimes I feel like I'm in a play, and I've forgotten my lines."

The children came. Daniel, then Sofia. She spoke to them in Spanish, sang them the songs her grandmother sang, filled the house with bright textiles from the markets back home.

In the kitchen, she found something like peace. *Baleadas* on Saturday mornings—flour tortillas stretched thin, stuffed with refried beans and crumbled *queso seco. Sopa de caracol* when someone was sick. The smells transported her back to her mother's kitchen, the radio playing *punta,* her grandmother's hands shaping masa.

But the children answered in English. They loved *baleadas* the way they loved pizza—another food, nothing more. They didn't know the songs were lullabies their great-grandmother had sung during the war.

"I'm raising Americans," Lucía said. "That's what I wanted for them. But sometimes I look at them and think: they'll never know who I was before."

The PTA started as distraction. Volunteering for bake sales, chaperoning field trips. But she noticed things the other mothers didn't—the kids who came to school without breakfast, the parents who never showed up because they were working two jobs, the way certain teachers called on certain children less.

She started asking questions. Polite questions. *Has anyone thought about a Spanish option for the newsletter? What about a breakfast program for families who need it?*

Some people welcomed her. Others did not.

Barbara Whitman caught her after a meeting once— Barbara with her highlighted hair and her Lexus and her smile that never quite reached her eyes.

"Lucía, I admire your enthusiasm. I really do." She touched Lucía's arm in that way that wasn't friendly. "But you're still relatively new to how we do things here. Maybe spend some time observing before you try to change everything?"

Lucía felt her face go hot. "I have a university degree. I've organized events that raised thousands of dollars. I've lived in three countries."

Barbara's smile didn't waver. "Of course. I just meant—you know. The culture here is different."

That night, Lucía sat in the dark kitchen after everyone was asleep. She thought about what Barbara really meant. *You're not one of us. You never will be.*

She ran for PTA board the next month. Won by twelve votes.

Her proudest achievement was supposed to be the charity drive. Six months of planning—spreadsheets, donor calls, venue negotiations. A resource fair for immigrant families. Legal aid, healthcare screenings, ESL information, winter coats for kids.

The day of the event, the community center buzzed. Families streamed through the doors—Salvadoran, Ethiopian, Vietnamese, Mexican. Children darted between tables. The air smelled of coffee and donated pastries.

Lucía moved through the crowd in her good silk blouse, the earrings David had given her for their anniversary. She translated for an elderly man struggling with a housing form. She directed a Somali mother toward the health screening table. She felt, for the first time in years, like she was doing something that mattered.

Then she saw the young woman.

Guatemalan, maybe twenty-two. Two small children clutching her legs. Eyes that looked older than her face.

Lucía approached her. "Can I help you find something?"

The woman looked at her—looked at the silk blouse, the earrings, the highlighted hair Lucía had gotten last week because David said it looked nice. Looked at her the way Lucía used to look at Sarah.

"Thank you," the woman said, in careful English. "You are very kind."

And Lucía understood. To this woman, she was one of *them*. The Americans. The people on the other side of the table.

She finished the event in a fog. Smiled, directed, translated. Drove home in silence.

That night, she couldn't sleep. She lay in the dark next to David and thought: *When did this happen? When did I cross over?*

She didn't know whether to feel proud or ashamed. She had become what her parents wanted—safe, successful, American. But something had been lost in the crossing, and she couldn't name what it was.

She still called her mother every Sunday. The connection was always bad—delays, static, her mother's voice fading in and out like a radio signal.

"*Mija*, you sound tired."

"I'm fine, Mamá. How's your knee?"

"The same. Your brother says hello. The baby is walking now—did I send you the video?"

These calls were the thread that held her to who she used to be. But every year the thread felt thinner. Her mother's life was there—the broken pipes, the neighbor's accordion, the cousin's quinceañera. Lucía's life was here—the PTA meetings, the soccer games, the slow erosion of her accent.

"Sometimes I think about visiting," she told me. "But every time I go, I feel like a tourist. The streets look smaller. Everyone treats me like a guest. My old room is a storage closet now."

She was quiet for a moment.

"And if I stayed too long, I'd miss Daniel's soccer tournament. Sofia's ballet recital. The PTA budget meeting." She laughed, but it wasn't happy. "My American life doesn't pause just because I want to go home."

It was late afternoon. The light through the windows had gone golden, and soon she'd have to leave for school pickup.

"Can I tell you something?" she said. "Something I've never told anyone?"

I nodded.

"Sometimes, when the house is empty—David at work, kids at school—I put on music. *Punta.* Garifuna drums. The kind of music my grandmother used to play when she was cooking." She smiled, almost shy. "I turn it up loud. So loud the windows shake. And I dance."

She mimed it—hips moving, arms raised, a gesture that belonged to a different woman in a different life.

"No one watching. No one judging. Not David's wife, not the PTA mom, not the immigrant success story. Just... Lucía. The girl from Colonia Moderna who used to dance in her grandmother's kitchen."

She looked at the family photos on the wall. Disney World. Christmas morning. A Potomac sunset.

"That's when I remember who I am. Or who I was. Or—"
She shook her head. "I don't know. Maybe both."

———

She stood and stretched. "I have to get the kids. Daniel has soccer, Sofia has ballet, and I still haven't figured out what to make for dinner that isn't chicken nuggets."

At the door, she paused.

"You know what my mother told me, last time we talked? She said, 'Lucía, stop feeling sorry for yourself. You wanted a different life, and you got one. Now live it.'"

She pulled on her jacket—North Face, practical—and grabbed her keys.

"She's right. She's always right. That's the thing about mothers."

Through the window, I watched her walk to the minivan. She opened the door, then stopped. Stood there for a moment, looking at nothing—the empty street, the identical lawns, the quiet that she once told me felt like a weight.

She said something I couldn't hear. Maybe a prayer. Maybe a name. Maybe just the word for home.

Then she got in, started the engine, and pulled out of the driveway—off to collect her children, sit in the carpool line, and continue the work of holding two lives inside one body.

5. Isabella

The shot wasn't right. Isabella could feel it—something in the way the afternoon light fell across the subject's face, too flat, too even. She held up her hand.

"Hold on. Marcos, can we get the bounce on the left side? I want to see the shadow under her cheekbone."

The crew adjusted. Washington Heights hummed around them—Dominican Spanish from the corner bodega, the rattle of the M4 bus, a man selling *piraguas* from a cart painted the colors of the Puerto Rican flag. Isabella had chosen this block specifically: the way the fire escapes created leading lines, the mural of Celia Cruz on the brick wall behind them, the light that came through the gap between buildings at exactly 3:47 p.m.

She looked through the viewfinder again. Better. The woman sitting on the plastic chair—Doña Carmen, seventy-three, from Puebla—had a face that caught light like landscape. Forty years in this neighborhood. Raised four children in a two-bedroom apartment. Buried a husband. Watched the block change around her.

"Okay," Isabella said. "Whenever you're ready."

Doña Carmen began to speak—about the bakery she'd owned on 181st Street, the one that closed last year when the rent tripled. Isabella kept the camera steady, but part of her mind was already editing: this shot dissolving into archival footage of the old storefront, then cutting to the luxury condo that stood there now. The juxtaposition would say what words couldn't.

This was how she saw the world. In frames, in cuts, in the space between images where meaning lived.

"I never planned to come to the United States," Isabella told me later, after the crew had wrapped for the day. We sat in a coffee shop on St. Nicholas Avenue, her equipment bags piled in the corner. "It was an accident. A lottery. Literally."

She was from Montevideo—the south side, near the Rambla, where the Río de la Plata stretched to the horizon like a brown ocean. Her father managed a shoe store; her mother taught piano. A middle-class family in a small country squeezed between giants.

"Uruguay is the country people forget exists," she said, smiling. "Argentina on one side, Brazil on the other, and us in the middle—three million people drinking *mate* and pretending we're European."

She'd discovered film at nineteen, at the Cinemateca Uruguaya—a cramped theater that showed Buñuel and Fellini and the Argentine New Wave. She remembered the first film that broke her open: *La Ciénaga*, Lucrecia Martel's humid, suffocating portrait of a family falling apart.

"I walked out of that theater and I knew. Not just that I wanted to make films—but that film could do something. It could make you feel what someone else felt. It could put you inside a life."

She enrolled in film school in Montevideo, scraping together tuition by working at her uncle's restaurant. She made short films on borrowed cameras—documentary sketches of the *murga* performers during Carnival, the old men playing chess in Plaza Independencia, the workers at the port.

"Small things," she said. "But I was learning to see."

Then came Valentina.

"We met at a screening. She was a photographer—worked for one of the newspapers." Isabella's voice softened. "Three years. We talked about making work together, maybe moving to Buenos Aires where there was more of a scene. We had plans."

She didn't say what ended it. I didn't ask. But I understood that when she entered the green card lottery in 2009, she was twenty-four years old, heartbroken, and looking for an exit.

"I didn't think I'd win. The odds are—what, one in a hundred? Less? I filled out the form online, uploaded a photo, and forgot about it."

Six months later, an envelope arrived. She was sitting in her apartment—the one she'd shared with Valentina before Valentina moved out—surrounded by half-finished scripts and dead plants she kept forgetting to water.

"I opened it, and there were these words in English: *Congratulations, you have been selected.* I read it three times. I thought it was a scam."

It wasn't. Out of millions of applicants, the algorithm had chosen her. Random. Arbitrary. A life-altering decision made by a computer in a government building she'd never see.

"That's the thing about the lottery," Isabella said. "It's not about merit. It's not about who deserves it. It's just—luck. Stupid, dumb luck." She shook her head. "Sometimes I think about all the people who applied that year who didn't win. Who were just as desperate, just as talented, just as ready to leave. And I got the golden ticket because a random number generator picked my name."

She paused.

"I've never figured out how to feel about that."

New York, 2010. She arrived in January, the worst possible month—gray skies, black snow, a cold that cut through every coat she owned.

"I had a suitcase and three thousand dollars. That was it. I found a room in a apartment in Jackson Heights—six people, one bathroom. My roommates were from Ecuador, Bangladesh, Korea. None of us spoke each other's languages. We communicated in broken English and hand gestures."

Film school was a blur of debt and exhaustion. She worked mornings at a coffee shop, classes in the afternoon, editing borrowed equipment at night. Her English was shaky; she missed jokes, misread social cues, spent whole lectures lost.

"I called my mother one night—I'd been here maybe six weeks. I was sitting on the floor because we didn't have enough chairs, and I was crying. I couldn't stop. I missed the Rambla, the smell of the river, the way the light looked in winter back home. I told her I wanted to come back."

"What did she say?"

Isabella smiled. "She said, 'You didn't leave to give up. You left to become something.' And then she told me the *chivito* at the corner place still wasn't as good as my grandmother's, and somehow that made me feel better."

She found a mentor—Andrés, another Uruguayan, twenty years older, who'd been making documentaries in New York since the eighties. He'd shot films about AIDS activism, labor organizing, the Salvadoran community in Long Island.

"He told me: 'You're an outsider here. That's your advantage. You see things Americans can't see because they're too close.' He was the first person who made me feel like my perspective wasn't a handicap—it was a gift."

Her first real documentary took two years. *Las Voces de Corona*—a portrait of Latino immigrants in Queens, their work and worship and waiting.

"I spent months in that neighborhood. Not filming—just being there. Going to Mass, eating at the *loncheras*, sitting in living rooms while people watched *telenovelas*. You can't just show up with a camera. You have to earn the right to point it at someone."

She told me about Doña Rosa—not the same as Doña Carmen, but similar, the kind of woman who became invisible in official accounts but held whole communities together. Doña Rosa ran an informal daycare out of her apartment: fifteen children, no license, fifty dollars a week per kid.

"She let me film her for six months. Her whole life—the mornings when mothers dropped off their kids before the subway, the afternoons when she cooked *arroz con pollo* for all of them, the nights when she was so tired she fell asleep in front of the TV."

The film premiered at a small festival in Brooklyn. Then a larger one. Then Tribeca.

"And suddenly people were calling me. Grants, commissions, invitations. It happened so fast."

She paused, stirring her coffee.

"You know what I remember most about that time? A few months after the film came out, I went back to Corona to visit Doña Rosa. I wanted to show her the reviews, tell her about the awards. And she was—" Isabella stopped. "She was exactly the same. Still running the daycare. Still tired. Still struggling to pay rent. I had built my career on her story, and nothing in her life had changed."

She looked at me directly.

"That's the thing nobody tells you about documentary. You take someone's life and turn it into art, and then you leave. You move on to the next project. But they're still there, living it. Sometimes I wonder if I'm any different from the journalists who parachute into a crisis, get their footage, and disappear."

I asked what she'd learned, in the years since.

"To stay in touch. To give back when I can—money, connections, whatever. To ask permission, always, and to accept when people say no." She set down her cup. "I turned down a project last year. A streaming service wanted me to make something about the border—kids in cages, all of it. Big budget. But they wanted it fast, they wanted it dramatic, and they didn't want to hear about spending a year building relationships with families. They wanted trauma on a timeline."

She shook her head.

"I'm not interested in poverty porn. I'm not interested in making Americans feel sad for an hour and then forget. If I'm going to tell someone's story, it has to mean something—to them, not just to the audience."

The light through the coffee shop window had gone golden. Rush hour outside—the roar of traffic, someone's car radio playing bachata.

"Do you miss Uruguay?"

"Every day." She said it without hesitation. "I miss the Rambla on Sunday mornings, everyone out walking with their *termo* and *mate*. I miss *asado* with my family, my father arguing about politics, my mother playing Piazzolla on the piano. I miss how small it is—how you can drive two hours and be somewhere completely different, and still everyone knows everyone."

She went back once a year, when she could afford it. Her parents were older now; her father had retired.

"My mother asks when I'm coming home for good. I don't know what to tell her. My life is here now. My work is here. But part of me is still on that Rambla, watching the water."

She pulled out her phone, showed me a photo: the Río de la Plata at dusk, the sky going pink and orange, a figure silhouetted against the water.

"Valentina took this. Years ago." She looked at it for a moment, then put the phone away. "We're friends now. She's married, has a kid. Lives in Barcelona. Sometimes I wonder what would have happened if I'd stayed. If we'd stayed together."

She shrugged—not dismissive, just accepting.

"But I wouldn't have made these films. I wouldn't have found this work. Sometimes you have to lose one life to find another."

We walked back to the set. The crew was prepping for the final shot of the day—Doña Carmen walking down the block where her bakery used to be, past the new condo, not looking at it.

"What do you want people to feel when they watch this?" I asked.

Isabella considered the question.

"I want them to see her. Not as a symbol, not as a statistic—as a person. A woman who built something with her hands, and then watched it disappear. I want them to understand that her story is this city's story. That every time a building goes up, something else comes down."

The light was fading—that blue-gray moment before sunset that cinematographers call magic hour.

"Places, everyone," Isabella called out. "Carmen, whenever you're ready. Just walk like you're coming home from the market. Don't think about the camera."

The old woman rose from her chair, smoothed her housedress, and began to walk. Isabella watched through the viewfinder as Carmen moved down the block, past the mural, past the new construction, her shadow long on the pavement.

"Beautiful," Isabella murmured, more to herself than anyone. "Hold there. Just like that."

The camera kept rolling. Washington Heights kept moving around them—the bus, the *piragua* cart, someone's abuela calling a child inside for dinner. All of it, the whole living city, held for a moment inside the frame.

Then Isabella called "Cut," and lowered the camera, and stood there looking at the street with her own eyes—seeing it first as footage, then as light, then as the place where she'd chosen to spend her life, making visible the people who might otherwise disappear.

6. José

The conference room had that particular Silicon Valley smell—recycled air, cold brew, and the faint desperation of people trying to seem relaxed. José Martínez sat at the long table with eleven other people, all of them watching a slide that read "Inclusive Excellence: Building Teams That Reflect Our Values."

He was the only Latino in the room. The only immigrant. One of three people of color, if you counted Priya from Legal and David from Sales, who was half-Korean but had grown up in Connecticut and sometimes forgot which half.

The facilitator—a white woman named Kendra with a consulting firm's worth of confidence—clicked to the next slide. "Now, let's talk about microaggressions in the workplace. Can anyone share an example they've witnessed?"

Silence. José watched his colleagues shift in their ergonomic chairs. No one wanted to go first. No one wanted to admit they'd seen anything, because admitting meant acknowledging, and acknowledging meant responsibility.

He could fill the silence. He had stories—years of them. The manager who'd praised his English. The recruiter who'd assumed he was the IT guy. The colleague who'd asked, genuinely curious, whether Colombia was "near Mexico." The time someone had asked if his "partner" was short for "business partner," and he'd had to decide, in the space of a breath, whether to correct them.

But José stayed quiet. He'd learned that these trainings weren't really about changing anything. They were about documentation. About the company being able to say they'd tried.

Kendra waited another beat, then filled the silence herself with a hypothetical. José tuned out, watching the San Francisco fog press against the window, thinking about how far he was from Bogotá.

He'd grown up in Chapinero, a neighborhood that had become the closest thing Bogotá had to a gay district—though when he was a child, it was just home. His father sold auto parts; his mother taught at a Catholic school. They lived in an apartment building with a doorman named Héctor who knew everyone's business and kept most of it to himself.

José knew he was different before he had words for it. At twelve, he understood. At fifteen, he told his sister, Camila, and she'd hugged him and said, "I know, *bobo*. I've always known."

His parents were harder.

"It's not that they rejected me," José told me, when we finally sat down to talk—not at the conference, but later, at a café in the Mission, the kind of place with oat milk and fifteen-dollar salads. "It's that they didn't know what to do with the information. My mother cried. My father just... went quiet. For weeks. Like I'd given him a puzzle he couldn't solve."

They never kicked him out. They never stopped loving him. But something shifted—a carefulness that hadn't been there before, a way of not quite looking at him when certain topics came up. When he brought home a boyfriend for the first time, his mother set an extra plate at the table and made conversation about the weather. His father shook the boy's hand and then found a reason to leave the room.

"In Colombia, you can be gay now. Legally, things have changed. But the *machismo*—" José shook his head. "It's in the walls. It's in the way people look at you on the street. My cousin came out a few years after me, and his father didn't speak to him for two years. Two years. So I consider myself lucky. But lucky isn't the same as accepted."

He met Sebastián in his last year of university. They were both studying computer science at Los Andes—Sebastián a year ahead, already talking about graduate school in the States.

"He was the first person who made me feel like I could have everything," José said. "The career, the relationship, the life. He made it seem possible."

They dated for two years. When Sebastián got into Stanford, he asked José to apply too.

"I wasn't sure I could get in. My grades were good, but Stanford?" José laughed. "In Bogotá, that felt like the moon. But Sebastián believed in me. He said, 'You're smarter than half the people there. You just don't know it yet.'"

José applied. He got in. And in the fall of 2011, they moved to California together—two Colombian boys in a studio apartment in Palo Alto, sharing a mattress on the floor because they couldn't afford a bed frame.

"Those first months were magic," José said. "Hard, but magic. We were broke, we were exhausted, we were completely lost. But we had each other."

It didn't last.

"Grad school does something to people. The pressure, the competition—it brings out things you didn't know were there." He paused, stirring his coffee. "Sebastián started pulling away. He was stressed, I was stressed, and instead of leaning on each other, we just... stopped talking. Really talking. By the end of the first year, we were roommates. By the second year, we were strangers."

They broke up the week before finals. Sebastián moved out. José stayed in the apartment alone, surrounded by the furniture they'd bought together, wondering if he'd made a mistake coming here at all.

"I thought about leaving. Going back to Bogotá, starting over. But I'd already given up so much to be here. My family, my friends, my whole life. I couldn't go back with nothing to show for it."

He finished his degree. He got a job offer. He got his H-1B visa. He stayed.

"People talk about tech like it's this meritocracy," José said. "Like the best code wins, and everything else is irrelevant. But that's not how it works. Not if you're brown. Not if you're an immigrant. Not if you're gay."

He'd worked at three companies since grad school—names I'd recognize, names on buildings and billboards. At each one, the pattern was the same.

"They hire you because you check a box. 'Latino engineer'—that's a two-fer. They put you on the diversity page of the website, they fly you to conferences to sit on panels. And then you go back to your desk, and you're still the only one. Still explaining where Colombia is. Still watching people's faces when you mention your boyfriend."

I asked if it had gotten better.

"In some ways. I'm senior now. I have power—real power. I can hire people, mentor people, push for change from inside." He paused. "But the higher you go, the lonelier it gets. The rooms get whiter. The conversations get more careful. And you start to wonder: Am I changing the system, or is the system changing me?"

He told me about a meeting last year. His company was launching a new initiative—"Diversity in Engineering," complete with a budget and a press release. José was asked to lead it.

"I was flattered. For about five minutes. Then I realized what they actually wanted. They wanted my face. My story. They wanted to say, 'Look, we have a gay Latino running our diversity program.' But when I asked for real resources—pipeline programs, retention support, bias training that wasn't just a box to check—suddenly the budget was tight. Suddenly there were 'competing priorities.'"

He smiled, but it didn't reach his eyes.

"I took the role anyway. Because if I didn't, someone else would—someone who wouldn't push. Someone who'd be happy with the press release." He shrugged. "Maybe that makes me complicit. Maybe I'm just telling myself a story to feel better about it. I don't know anymore."

There were good things too. He wanted me to know that.

"I run a mentorship program. *Código Diverso.* We pair engineers with students from underrepresented backgrounds—first-gen, immigrants, LGBTQ kids who don't see themselves in this industry."

He told me about Juana, a young woman from Medellín who'd grown up in a *comuna*, one of the hillside neighborhoods that tourists never saw. She'd taught herself to code on a secondhand laptop, applied to the program on a whim.

"When I first talked to her, she kept apologizing. For her English, for her questions, for taking up my time. I told her: 'You don't have to apologize for existing. You have just as much right to be here as anyone.'" He paused. "She's at Google now. Sometimes she texts me pictures of her badge, like she still can't believe it."

This was what kept him going, he said. Not the panels, not the press releases. The individual people. The ones he could actually help.

"You can't save everyone. You can't fix the system by yourself. But you can hold the door open for the person behind you. That's something. That has to be something."

I asked about his personal life. Whether he'd found someone since Sebastián.

José was quiet for a moment.

"I date. Sometimes. But it's hard. The apps are—" He made a face. "You know how it is. Everyone's looking for something specific. Tall, masc, white. If you're Latino, you're 'spicy.' If you're Asian, you're—whatever stereotype they've got. It's exhausting."

He'd had a few relationships. Nothing that lasted.

"I think part of it is me. I give so much to work, to the mentorship, to being the 'diverse voice' in every room. By the time I get home, I don't have anything left." He looked out the window. "Sometimes I wonder if that's a choice, or just a story I tell myself."

He still talked to Sebastián occasionally. They were friendly now—the kind of friendly that came after enough time had passed.

"He's married. To a guy he met at Stanford, actually. A white guy from Connecticut." José laughed. "They have a dog. A golden retriever. The whole thing."

Was he jealous?

"No. Maybe. I don't know." He shrugged. "I'm happy for him. I'm happy for myself, too. I've built something here. It's just... different from what I imagined."

The fog had lifted by the time we left the café. The Mission was coming alive—murals and taco trucks and the distant thump of music from somewhere down the block. José walked with me toward the BART station, hands in his jacket pockets.

"You know what I miss most about Bogotá?" he said. "The noise. Here, everyone wears headphones. Everyone's in their own bubble. In Chapinero, you couldn't walk down the street without someone calling out to you—a neighbor, a vendor, the guy who fixed your shoes. It was loud and chaotic and sometimes annoying, but you were never alone. You were part of something."

He stopped at the corner.

"Here, I have to build that from scratch. Every connection, every community—I have to make it happen. Nobody's going to hand it to me."

We shook hands. He had another meeting—he always had another meeting—and I watched him walk away, disappearing into the crowd of people staring at their phones, each of them alone in their own way.

I thought about what he'd said. About holding doors open. About not being able to fix the system, but showing up anyway. About the gap between the version of yourself you put on panels and the version that goes home at night to an empty apartment.

José Martínez: gay, Colombian, immigrant, engineer, mentor, token, advocate, survivor. All of it true. None of it the whole story.

That night, I looked him up online. The company headshot: professional smile, company logo behind him. The conference bio: "José Martínez is a passionate advocate for diversity in tech." The LinkedIn profile: five hundred connections, a dozen endorsements, a life reduced to bullet points.

None of it mentioned Sebastián. None of it mentioned the apartment in Palo Alto with the mattress on the floor. None of it mentioned what it cost to be the only one in the room, year after year, and keep showing up anyway.

But I knew now. And maybe that was enough—one more person who knew the real story, underneath the slides and the press releases and the carefully curated feed.

One more person who saw him.

7. Gabriela and Cecilia

Cecilia

She watched her daughter cross the stage in a purple gown, and she thought: *I carried you through the desert. I carried you in my arms when you were four years old and the water was gone and I thought we would die.*

The auditorium was full of families—white families, mostly, with their flowers and their cameras and their easy smiles. Cecilia sat in her best dress, the one Gabriela had helped her pick out at the mall in Yakima, and she clutched her bouquet so tight the stems bent.

Gabriela Torres.

The name echoed through the speakers. Her daughter. Her *mija*. Walking across that stage like she belonged there, like she had always belonged there.

Cecilia's hands were shaking. She hid them in her lap so no one would see.

Gabriela

I don't remember Mexico. Not really.

I remember impressions. The smell of cilantro. My grandmother's hands, rough and warm. A courtyard with a lemon tree. But when I try to hold the memories, they slip away like water.

What I remember is the crossing. Fragments. The back of a truck, the smell of gasoline and sweat. My mother's voice singing in the dark. The scratch of desert brush against my legs. Thirst so deep it felt like my throat was closing.

I was four. Old enough to walk, too young to understand. My mother carried my baby brother, and I held onto her skirt, and we walked through the night toward lights I couldn't see.

She tells me I never cried. I don't know if that's true or if it's the story she needs to believe.

Cecilia

In Guanajuato, I finished third grade. Then my father said: *enough*. Girls don't need school. Girls need to work.

I was eight years old. I worked the fields until I was nineteen and married. I worked the fields until I had three children and no money and a husband who drank. I worked the fields until I looked at my daughter—my Gabriela, so smart, always asking questions—and I thought: *not her. She will have more than this.*

My cousins had gone north. They sent letters about jobs, about schools, about a place where your children could become something. I saved money for two years, hiding pesos in a coffee can under the stove. When I had enough for the *coyote*, I took my children and I left.

I did not say goodbye to my mother. I was afraid she would talk me out of it. I was afraid I would stay.

Gabriela

The Yakima Valley is high desert—brown hills, sagebrush, irrigation canals cutting green lines through the dust. In summer, the temperature hits a hundred degrees and the air smells like baked earth and pesticide. In fall, the orchards turn heavy with apples, and the whole valley fills with workers moving through the rows.

That's where we landed. My mother's cousins had a trailer outside Sunnyside, and they took us in. Five of us in two rooms, and my mother started work the next week.

Apple season runs September through November. You wake before dawn, drive to the orchard in the dark, and climb ladders until your shoulders scream. The picking bag hangs from your neck—forty pounds when it's full—and you learn to move fast because you're paid by the bin, not the hour. Twelve hours later, you drive home in the dark, eat whatever's quick, and fall asleep before your head hits the pillow.

My mother did this for fifteen years.

I did it too, summers and weekends, until I was old enough to get other jobs. But I never forgot the weight of that bag. The way your fingers crack and bleed. The way you stop feeling your back after the first few hours because the pain becomes background noise.

Cecilia

People ask me: was it worth it?

I show them my hands. The knuckles swollen, the skin thick and cracked. I cannot make a fist anymore. The joints hurt when it rains.

These hands picked a million apples. These hands paid for my daughter's books, her clothes, her bus tickets to Seattle. These hands built her life.

Sí, I tell them. *It was worth it.*

Gabriela

I was seventeen when DACA passed. I remember exactly where I was: the living room of our trailer, watching the news on the little TV my mother had bought at a garage sale. President Obama was speaking, and I didn't understand all the words, but I understood enough.

Deferred action. Work permits. A chance.

My mother was in the kitchen. I called to her, and she came out wiping her hands on a dishcloth, and we stood there together watching. When it was over, she said: "What does it mean?"

I said: "It means I can stay."

She started to cry. I had never seen my mother cry—not during the crossing, not during the years of work, not when my father stopped sending money. But she cried then, standing in our living room with the dishcloth still in her hands.

Cecilia

I did not understand DACA. I still do not understand it, not really. I know it is not a green card. I know it is not permanent. I know that every two years, Gabriela has to apply again, has to pay the fee, has to wait and hope.

I know that it can be taken away.

When the news talks about immigration, I leave the room. I cannot watch. Gabriela tells me not to worry, that she will be fine, but I see her face when she checks her phone. I see the way her shoulders tighten when a notification comes through.

She thinks I don't notice. But a mother notices everything.

Gabriela

The renewal process costs $495. Every two years, you gather your documents—proof of continuous residence, proof of education, proof that you are still the same person who was approved before—and you send them in and you wait.

The wait is the worst part. Eight weeks, sometimes twelve. You check your case status online, refreshing the page like it might change if you look hard enough. You go to class, you go to work, you live your life. But underneath everything, there's this hum of fear. A frequency you can't turn off.

In 2017, when the administration announced they were ending DACA, I was in the library at UW, studying for a midterm. I felt my phone buzz, saw the news alert, and my vision went white at the edges. I couldn't breathe. I sat there for ten minutes, staring at nothing, while the world continued around me.

A girl at the next table asked if I was okay. I said yes. I smiled. I went back to studying.

What else was I supposed to do?

Cecilia

When Gabriela left for college, I drove her to Seattle myself. Four hours through the mountains, the pass so high my ears popped. I had never been to Seattle before. The buildings were so tall, the streets so crowded. I felt like I was in another country.

The campus was like a city. So many young people, so many buildings with names I couldn't pronounce. Gabriela showed me her dorm room—a little box with a bed and a desk—and I thought: *this is where she will live now. Without me.*

I helped her unpack. I made her bed with the sheets we had bought at Target, the ones with the purple flowers. When it was time to go, I held her for a long time. I said: "Call me. Every week."

She said: "I will, Mami."

I cried the whole drive home. Four hours through the mountains, and I could barely see the road.

Gabriela

I didn't fit in. I knew I wouldn't, but knowing didn't make it easier.

The other freshmen talked about their gap years, their AP classes, their parents who were lawyers and doctors and tech executives. They went to parties on Greek Row and complained about the dining hall food and planned spring break trips to Cabo.

I worked twenty hours a week at the library. I sent money home when I could. I called my mother every Sunday and translated the bills that came in the mail.

I tried a sorority rush, once. I stood in a room full of girls in sundresses, holding a plastic cup of lemonade, and someone asked me what my father did.

I said: "He's not around."

She said: "Oh, I'm so sorry." And then she moved on to someone else.

I didn't go back.

Cecilia

Gabriela called me crying, those first months. She said she didn't belong. She said everyone else knew things she didn't know—how to talk, how to dress, how to be.

I didn't know what to tell her. I had never been to college. I didn't know what a sorority was. I didn't know how to help her with her papers or her professors or her problems.

All I could say was: *you are strong. You have survived worse than this. Keep going.*

Sometimes that is not enough. But sometimes it is all a mother has.

Gabriela

Then I found CAMP.

The College Assistance Migrant Program. A room in Mary Gates Hall with fluorescent lights and mismatched chairs and a coffee maker that was always on.

I walked in for a meeting my first October, and the first thing I saw was a poster of Dolores Huerta on the wall. The first thing I heard was Spanish—real Spanish, not classroom Spanish, the kind my mother spoke. The first thing I smelled was someone's *abuela's* tamales, still warm in their foil.

There were fifteen students in that room, and all of them looked like me. Brown faces, tired eyes, the particular posture of people who had worked since they were young. Someone mentioned the apple harvest, and someone else groaned in recognition, and suddenly I was laughing—really laughing—for the first time since I'd arrived.

In CAMP, I wasn't the "diversity admit" or the "scholarship kid." I wasn't the girl who didn't know what a gap year was. I was Gabriela, daughter of farmworkers, first in her family to go to college, tired and scared and determined.

I was home.

Cecilia

She stopped crying on the phone. She started telling me
about her classes, her friends, her plans. She sounded like herself
again—like the little girl who always asked questions, who
always wanted to know more.

I could not give her what the other parents gave. I could
not help her with her homework. I could not visit on parents'
weekend because I could not take time off from work. I could
not explain the world she was living in because I had never lived
in it myself.

But I could listen. I could tell her I was proud. I could
remind her that she had walked through the desert when she
was four years old, and if she could do that, she could do
anything.

Gabriela

I graduated on a Saturday in June. The sun was out, the
mountains visible in the distance, the whole campus alive with
families.

My mother sat in the audience in her good dress, the one I
helped her pick out. She didn't understand the ceremony—the
Latin phrases, the academic regalia, the long speeches about
futures and possibilities. But when my name was called, she
stood up.

She stood up, and she clapped, and she didn't stop clapping
until I had crossed the entire stage.

After the ceremony, we walked to the car. My mother moved slowly—her knees hurt, her back hurt, fifteen years of orchards written into her body. I carried my diploma and my cap with *Sí Se Puede* written on top.

"Are you hungry?" she asked.

"Starving."

"Good. I brought *tamales*. They're in the cooler."

We sat in the parking lot, eating tamales out of foil wrappers, watching the other families stream past with their flowers and their balloons. My mother's hands shook a little when she unwrapped hers—the joints don't work like they used to.

"*Mija*," she said, after a while.

"Yes?"

"I am proud of you."

She said it simply, the way she says everything. No drama, no tears. Just the fact of it, laid out plain.

"I know, Mami."

"But I am also afraid."

I looked at her. She was staring out the windshield at the parking lot, at the families passing by.

"The DACA," she said. "It can go away."

"I know."

"What will you do?"

I didn't have an answer. I never have an answer. The policy shifts, the courts rule, the news alerts light up my phone, and every two years I send in my $495 and my documents and my hope.

"I don't know," I said. "But I'll figure it out. I always do."

She nodded. She wrapped up the rest of her tamal and put it back in the cooler.

"Okay," she said. "*Vámonos.* Four hours to home."

She started the car. I put my diploma in the backseat, between the cooler and the box of my things. We pulled out of the parking lot and onto the freeway, heading east toward the mountains.

The Cascades rose up ahead of us, green and white and impossibly tall. On the other side was the valley—the brown hills, the orchards, the trailer where I grew up. My mother drove with both hands on the wheel, the way she always does, careful and steady.

I watched the road unspool ahead of us and thought about the future. Graduate school, maybe. A job in public health. A chance to help people like us, people who work in the fields and live in the shadows and hope their children will have more.

But first: the drive home. The mountains. My mother beside me, her ruined hands on the wheel.

For now, that was enough.

8. Maria Cristina

The map hung opposite her desk so she would see it every day. *Descripción de las Indias Occidentales*, 1601—the Americas as Spain imagined them, vast and conquerable, the coastlines still uncertain. Her father had given it to her when she accepted the position at the university. "So you remember where you come from," he said. She had hung it as a reminder of something else.

Maria Cristina Lopez looked up from her laptop as a knock came at the open door. A young woman stood in the frame, backpack over one shoulder, a worn copy of *Borderlands/La Frontera* clutched against her chest.

"Professor Lopez? I'm Alejandra. From your Cultural Identity seminar."

"*Sí, claro.* Come in." Maria Cristina gestured to the chair across from her desk. "Office hours don't officially start for another fifteen minutes, but you're here now."

Alejandra sat on the edge of the seat, not settling in. Maria Cristina had learned to read this posture—the students who came with questions they'd been carrying for weeks, waiting for the right moment.

"What's on your mind?"

"I've been thinking about the reading. About Gloria Anzaldúa." Alejandra turned the book over in her hands. "She writes about being *mestiza*, about straddling cultures. And I get it—I mean, I live it. My parents are from Oaxaca. I grew up in East Boston."

Maria Cristina nodded, waiting.

"But then I look at the syllabus, and I look at the department website, and I see your bio." Alejandra's voice was careful, but direct. "It says you're from Barcelona."

There it was. Maria Cristina had been waiting for this conversation for six years, since her first semester in this office. Some semesters it came in whispers—*She's not really one of us*—and some semesters it came like this, face to face, from a student brave enough to ask.

"That's right," Maria Cristina said. "I was born in Barcelona. My parents are both Spanish academics."

Alejandra met her eyes. "So what do you know about being Latina in America?"

The question hung in the air, and Maria Cristina let it hang. She could feel the old defenses rising—*I've dedicated my career to this, I've published twenty papers, I speak the language*—but she had learned, over time, that those answers only made things worse.

"I don't know what it's like to grow up Latina in America," she said finally. "I can't. I arrived here at twenty-four with a fellowship and a European passport. I've never been stopped at a border. I've never worried about my family's papers."

Alejandra's posture shifted slightly, listening now rather than challenging.

"What I know," Maria Cristina continued, "is what Spain did. The *encomienda*. The missions. The centuries of extraction that built Barcelona's palaces and left Latin America with the scars." She gestured toward the map on the wall. "My ancestors drew those lines. Decided who was human and who was property. That history lives in me whether I want it to or not."

"So why teach this?" Alejandra asked. "Why not—I don't know—Spanish literature? Something safer?"

Maria Cristina smiled, a tired smile that acknowledged the question's weight. "Because Dr. Elena Rueda asked me the same thing, twenty years ago. She was my mentor in graduate school. Colombian, raised in Bogotá, came to the States with nothing. And she saw something in me that I couldn't see yet—that my discomfort with Spain's history could be a tool, not just a burden."

She reached for a framed photograph on her desk: a younger Maria Cristina standing between two women outside an ivy-covered building, all three squinting into the sun.

"Dr. Rueda on the left. Dr. Lucero on the right—my department chair for many years. They both pushed me to claim this work, even when I felt like a fraud. *Especially* when I felt like a fraud."

Alejandra studied the photo. "And you don't feel like a fraud anymore?"

"I feel it less," Maria Cristina admitted. "But the doubt never disappears entirely. It shows up in different forms. A colleague suggesting that my 'outsider perspective' makes me 'objective'—as if my distance from the material is an asset rather than a limitation. A conference panel where I'm the only one without a family story of crossing borders."

She set the photo down. "What I've learned is that acknowledging the limitation is part of the work. I don't speak for the experience. I teach *about* it. I create space for students like you to speak for yourselves."

Alejandra was quiet for a moment. Then: "My *abuela* used to say that Spaniards always acted like they owned the place."

Maria Cristina laughed—a real laugh, surprised out of her. "Your grandmother sounds like a wise woman."

"She also said that anyone who sits with you at the table is family, eventually." Alejandra's expression softened, just slightly. "I'm not there yet. But I appreciate you not pretending."

"I could never pretend. Not in this room." Maria Cristina nodded toward the map. "That's why I keep it. My students deserve to know where I come from."

After Alejandra left, Maria Cristina sat with the conversation for a long moment. It never got easier, exactly, but it got clearer. She had stopped trying to prove she belonged. Belonging wasn't the point. The work was the point.

She thought about the first-generation students she had interviewed for her research, years ago now. Elena, who worked two jobs while carrying a full course load, who told her: "*Sometimes I feel like I'm living in two worlds. At home, I'm the dutiful daughter making tortillas with my abuela. At school, I'm debating Foucault.*" Miguel, whose mother had said: "*Tú eres nuestra esperanza, mijo. Sigue adelante.*" You are our hope, son. Keep going.

Some of those students had graduated, gone on to graduate school themselves, sent her notes from their own offices. Others had disappeared—one semester present, the next gone.

Deported. Dropped out. Overwhelmed. The ones she couldn't reach stayed with her longer than the successes.

There was David, who sat in the back row of her seminar for three weeks, never speaking, then stopped coming. She had emailed him, left voicemails, asked his advisor. Nothing. Months later she learned he'd been picked up by ICE at a traffic stop. Last she heard, he was back in Guatemala, the country he'd left when he was four years old.

She kept his paper in her desk drawer. *The Construction of Illegality in American Discourse.* Unfinished. Brilliant in its first five pages. She reread it sometimes when she needed to remember what was at stake.

The office hours line formed as it always did: Sophia, struggling with intersectionality, needing the concepts broken down into smaller pieces; Jason, brimming with an idea about reggaeton and pan-Latino identity that he couldn't quite articulate yet; Mei, an international student caught between her family's expectations and her own quiet ambitions.

Then Eduardo.

He sat down slowly, as if the chair might not hold him. First-generation. Scholarship student. The weight of his family's hopes visible in his shoulders.

"Professor Lopez, I don't know if I should be here."

Maria Cristina waited.

"Not in your office," he clarified. "Here. At this university. Sometimes I look around and everyone seems to know something I don't. Like there's a code nobody gave me."

"What do you think the code is?"

"I don't know." His voice dropped. "How to talk to professors. How to ask for things. When to speak up in class and when to stay quiet. My roommate's dad went here. His grandfather went here. He just *knows*."

Maria Cristina leaned forward. "Eduardo, look at me."

He did, reluctantly.

"The code is real. I won't lie to you and say it isn't. There are things you'll have to learn that your roommate absorbed without trying." She held his gaze. "But here's what your roommate will never have: the knowledge of what it costs to be here. The double vision of someone who sees the institution from the outside and the inside at the same time. That perspective is not a deficit. It's a tool."

Eduardo's jaw tightened. "It doesn't feel like a tool. It feels like I'm always translating."

"Yes," Maria Cristina said. "And translation is exhausting. I know. I've been translating between worlds for twenty years." She paused. "But translation is also a skill that most people never develop. You're building muscle that will serve you long after you leave this place."

He didn't look convinced. She hadn't expected him to—not yet. The doubt would take longer than one office hour to unwind.

"I can't promise you that it gets easy," she said. "But I can promise you that you earned your place here. Not because someone gave it to you. Because you fought for it. Don't let anyone—including yourself—tell you otherwise."

Eduardo nodded, slowly. "Can I come back next week?"

"*Siempre,*" Maria Cristina said. Always. "My door is open."

By late afternoon, the hallway had quieted. Most students were heading to the dining hall or the library. Maria Cristina gathered her notes for the next day's lecture, straightening the papers that had accumulated across her desk like sediment.

She caught sight of the photo again—Dr. Rueda, Dr. Lucero, herself in the middle, thirty years old and terrified, having just been offered the job she wasn't sure she deserved. Dr. Rueda had died three years ago. Dr. Lucero had retired last spring. Now Maria Cristina was the one with the office full of books, the one students came to with their questions and their doubts.

The lineage continued whether she felt ready for it or not.

A knock at the door. Another student, a face she didn't recognize, hesitant in the doorway.

"Is this Professor Lopez's office? I'm looking for the Cultural Identity seminar?"

Maria Cristina smiled and reached for a syllabus from the stack on her desk.

"You found it. Come in. Tell me your name."

The student stepped forward, and Maria Cristina did what she had always done, what Dr. Rueda had done for her, what she would keep doing until there was no one left to teach.

She began.

9. Francisco

The Morales family was deported on a Tuesday.

Francisco found out from a voicemail. He had been in court all morning on another case, phone silenced, and when he finally checked his messages there were seven—three from his paralegal, two from the family's pastor, one from a reporter, and one from Guadalupe Morales herself, recorded from the detention center at 6:47 a.m., her voice steady in a way that broke him.

"*Licenciado*, they're putting us on the plane today. I wanted to thank you for everything you did. Please don't blame yourself. You fought for us. God bless you."

He had fought for them for three years. Exposed the fraud in their original hearing. Filed every motion. Called in every favor. And in the end, a judge looked at the paperwork and decided that Guadalupe's fear of the cartel that had killed her brother was not specific enough, not documented enough, not *enough*.

She was going back to Michoacán with her two daughters. The girls had been six and eight when they arrived. Now they were nine and eleven, and they spoke better English than Spanish, and they were being sent to a country they barely remembered, to a town where their uncle had been shot in his own driveway.

Francisco sat in his car in the courthouse parking garage for twenty minutes. He did not cry. He had stopped crying years ago—not because the losses hurt less, but because there were too many of them, and if he cried for each one he would never stop.

Then he drove back to the office, because there were other families waiting.

His father had been the same way. Francisco understood this now, decades later—the way his father would come home from the office during the Allende years, exhausted but unable to stop, because there was always another worker who needed representation, another union facing retaliation, another case that couldn't wait.

"*Mira, Panchito*," his father said once, when Francisco was eight years old, sitting in the corner of the cramped office in Santiago while his father worked late. "You see these files? Each one is a family. A person with a name, with children, with a life. The law is just paper until someone fights to make it real."

That was 1972. Francisco remembered the hope of those years—Allende's voice on the radio, his mother's friends gathering in the kitchen to talk about what Chile could become. His parents were wealthy lawyers who could have stayed comfortable under any regime, but they had chosen a side. They defended workers. They believed in something.

Then came September 11, 1973.

Francisco was nine years old. He remembered the jets screaming over Santiago, the smoke rising from La Moneda, the presidential palace. He remembered his mother pulling him away from the window. He remembered, in the days that followed, the way adults stopped talking when children entered the room.

His father's colleague, Rodrigo Espinoza, disappeared three weeks after the coup. Rodrigo had been at their house for dinner the month before, had taught Francisco how to play chess, had laughed too loud and drunk too much wine. One morning he went to work and never came home. His wife called Francisco's parents, frantic. They made inquiries. They were told to stop asking questions.

Rodrigo's body was never found. His name appeared, years later, on the lists of the disappeared. By then Francisco was in law school in California, reading about his country's horrors in academic journals, learning the clinical language for what he had lived through as a child.

His parents stayed in Chile through the dictatorship—too prominent to disappear, too stubborn to leave, quietly defending political prisoners when they could, keeping their heads down when they couldn't. Francisco left in 1985, the year he turned twenty-one, with his father's blessing and his mother's tears. "Go," his father said. "Learn their laws. Then use them."

The irony was not lost on Francisco, then or now. He had fled to the country that orchestrated Pinochet's rise. He had learned law in the nation whose CIA had funded the coup, whose economists had designed the policies that gutted Chile's working class. And now he spent his days defending immigrants from that same country's enforcement apparatus.

"*Es una locura, po,*" he said sometimes, to no one in particular. It's madness. But madness was the only sane response to an insane system.

He had tried corporate law first. A big firm in Los Angeles, the kind of place where they measured success in billable hours and corner offices. He lasted two years.

The case that broke him was a class action—or rather, the defense against one. He was helping a corporation bury a lawsuit from workers who had been exposed to toxic chemicals. His job was to find procedural reasons to delay, to exhaust the plaintiffs' resources, to make justice too expensive to pursue.

One night, alone in the office at midnight, he found himself staring at a deposition transcript. A woman describing her husband's death from cancer, how he had coughed blood for months, how the company doctor kept telling him it was nothing. Francisco closed the file and walked out of the building. He never went back.

The Immigrant Defenders Law Center hired him a month later. The pay was a third of what he'd been making. The hours were worse. The office was a cramped suite with bad lighting and a coffee machine that worked half the time.

He had never been happier.

The waiting room was full when he arrived back from the courthouse. Three families, a young man alone, an elderly woman with a folder of documents she clutched like a talisman. His paralegal, Monica, caught his eye and tilted her head toward his office—*someone's waiting*.

Inside, a man sat in the client chair, work boots still dusty, a baseball cap turning in his hands. Beside him, a woman in scrubs—she must have come straight from a shift. Between them, a boy of maybe fifteen, staring at the floor.

"Mr. and Mrs. Delgado?" Francisco extended his hand. "I'm Francisco Herrera. Tell me what's happening."

The story was familiar. Twenty-two years in the country. Three children, all citizens. Arturo Delgado had been picked up at a job site last month—no warrant, just an ICE officer who decided to check papers. Now he had a removal order. The hearing was in six weeks.

"They said he has no case," Mrs. Delgado said, her voice tight with controlled panic. "The other lawyer we talked to, he said there's nothing to do."

"There's always something to do," Francisco said. "It may not be enough. I won't lie to you about the odds. But there's always something."

He spent an hour with them, going through Arturo's history, looking for anything—a crime he witnessed, a threat he received, family in danger back home. The son, Miguel, finally spoke up near the end.

"My dad coached my Little League team for six years. Everyone in the neighborhood knows him. Doesn't that matter?"

Francisco looked at the boy, saw the desperation beneath the question, the need to believe that goodness counted for something in the eyes of the law.

"It should matter," he said. "And we'll make sure the judge knows. But I have to be honest with you, Miguel. The system doesn't always work the way it should."

The boy's jaw tightened. He looked, for a moment, like he might cry. Then he nodded, once, and went back to staring at the floor.

That night, Francisco sat in his home office long after Elena and the kids had gone to bed. The Delgado file was open in front of him, but he wasn't reading it. He was thinking about Guadalupe Morales on that plane, her daughters beside her, flying toward a place where a cartel had already killed one member of their family.

He thought about Rodrigo Espinoza, who had taught him chess and disappeared into Pinochet's prisons. He thought about his father, working late into the night in Santiago, believing that the law could be made real.

The odds for Arturo Delgado were not good. Francisco had looked at enough cases to know. Twenty-two years of good behavior, three citizen children, a community that loved him— none of it created a legal right to stay. The law was not interested in goodness. The law was interested in categories, and Arturo had entered the country without permission in 2002, and that fact would follow him forever.

But there's always something to do.

Francisco pulled the file closer and began to read again, looking for the angle, the argument, the crack in the wall. Somewhere in these pages was a chance—small, maybe, but real. And if he found it, he would fight for it with everything he had, the way his father had fought, the way Dolores Huerta had fought, the way everyone who believed in justice had to fight, knowing that they would lose more than they won, and fighting anyway.

The house was quiet. The desk lamp made a small circle of light in the darkness.

He picked up his pen and began to write.

10. Elena

The call comes through at 11:47 p.m., the way it always does—Carlos waiting until the children are asleep, until the rates drop, until he's walked home from the school where he still teaches to the apartment where he now lives alone.

"*Mi amor.*" His voice arrives a half-second late, the lag that Elena has learned to wait for. "How are the kids?"

"Good. Alejandro got an A on his math test. He wanted to stay up to tell you, but—"

"It's late there. I know." A pause. "And Isabela?"

"She made a friend. A girl named Sophie, from her class. They're going to have a playdate this weekend."

"A playdate." Carlos repeats the English word like he's tasting something unfamiliar. "That's good. That's really good."

Elena sits on the edge of her bed in the apartment in Atlanta, the one she shares with her children and, on weekends, with another Venezuelan family whose mother works night shifts. The room is dark except for the glow of her phone. Three thousand miles away, Carlos is sitting somewhere too— she pictures him at the small table by the window, the one they bought together when they first married, back when Caracas was still a city where you could buy furniture without waiting in line for six hours.

"How are things there?" she asks, though she already knows the answer. Things there are the same. Things there are worse.

"The power was out for fourteen hours yesterday. I taught by candlelight." He laughs, but it's not a real laugh. "The students joke that we're preparing for the apocalypse. Maybe we are."

She wants to say: *Come. Please. I'll find a way.* But she's said it before, and he's answered before, and the conversation always ends in the same silence.

"Elena," he says, and something in his voice makes her grip the phone tighter. "I got a letter from the government. They're 'reviewing' my teaching credentials. Because of the union meetings."

Her stomach drops. "Carlos—"

"It's fine. It's probably nothing. They're just trying to scare people."

"It's not nothing. You know it's not nothing."

The lag stretches between them, longer than the satellite delay.

"I can't leave," he says finally. "You know I can't. If everyone leaves, who teaches the children? Who keeps the schools open?"

"The children who matter most are here," Elena says, and immediately wishes she could take it back. But it's true, and they both know it, and the silence that follows is the same silence that has lived between them for eighteen months.

"I should let you sleep," Carlos says.

"Carlos—"

"Kiss the kids for me. Tell Alejandro I'm proud of him."

"I will."

"*Te amo*, Elena."

"*Te amo.*"

The call ends. Elena sits in the dark for a long time, the phone still warm in her hand.

She made the decision on a Tuesday night in Caracas, standing in front of an empty pantry while her children slept in the next room.

It wasn't one thing. It was everything. It was Alejandro refusing to play outside after he saw the *colectivos* beat a protestor on their street. It was Isabela crying at the sound of helicopters, convinced they were coming to hurt them. It was Carlos coughing for weeks from an infection they couldn't afford medicine to treat. It was the morning Elena went to six pharmacies looking for antibiotics and came home with nothing.

She had known for months that they needed to leave. Carlos had known too, she thought, though he wouldn't say it. He believed in staying. He believed that if all the good people fled, Venezuela would have nothing left.

"We can wait it out," he kept saying. "Things will get better. They have to."

But things didn't get better. And one night, after the children were asleep, Elena told him she was taking them to the United States.

"You're leaving," he said. Not a question.

"I'm taking the children somewhere safe. You can come with us."

"You know I can't."

"You mean you won't."

Carlos looked at her, and she saw something in his face she had never seen before—not anger, exactly, but a kind of grief that went deeper than anger. "You're asking me to abandon everything I believe in."

"I'm asking you to choose your family."

"I am choosing my family. I'm choosing to fight for a country where our children can come home someday."

They argued for hours. They argued for days. In the end, nothing was resolved. Elena bought three plane tickets—herself, Alejandro, Isabela—and Carlos helped her pack, and on the morning they left he drove them to the airport and carried their suitcases to the curb and held each of his children so tightly that Isabela squirmed and said, "Papi, you're hurting me."

"I'm sorry," he said, releasing her. "I'm sorry, *mi cielo*."

He looked at Elena last. She waited for him to say something—to beg her to stay, to tell her she was wrong, to give her a reason to put down the suitcases and go home. But he didn't. He just looked at her with those dark eyes she had fallen in love with twenty years ago, and said: "Call me when you land."

"Come with us," she said. One last time.

He shook his head. "I can't."

She picked up the suitcases. She took her children's hands. She walked through the doors of Simón Bolívar International Airport and did not look back, because she knew that if she looked back she would not be able to keep walking.

The first months in Atlanta were a blur of shelters and food banks, of forms she couldn't read and systems she didn't understand. Her English was basic, her savings nearly gone by the time they landed. She had a cousin in Atlanta—a distant cousin, someone she barely knew—who let them stay on her couch for the first two weeks until Elena found a room in a house shared by three other immigrant families.

She learned about TPS from a woman at the community center, a legal aid worker named Maria who helped her fill out the paperwork. Temporary Protected Status. It meant she could work, could stay, could stop looking over her shoulder every time she saw a police car. It wasn't permanent, but it was something.

She took whatever jobs she could find. Cleaning offices at night. Stocking shelves at a grocery store. Translating documents for a lawyer who paid her in cash. The children went to school and came home speaking English words she didn't know, and she felt proud and also something else, something like loss, watching them become American while she remained something in between.

She called Carlos every week. Sometimes twice. The calls were expensive even on WhatsApp, and the connection was bad, and there was never enough time to say what needed to be said.

"The school is closing," he told her in November. "They say they can't afford to keep it open."

"What will you do?"

"I don't know. Maybe tutor. There are still families who want their children to learn."

"Carlos, please—"

"Don't, Elena. Please don't."

She stopped asking him to come. She stopped because asking hurt too much, and because his answer was always the same, and because she had started to wonder if he was right—if staying and fighting was the braver choice, and leaving was just running away.

By the second year, she had found a kind of rhythm. A job as an administrative assistant at a nonprofit that helped refugees. A small apartment, just two bedrooms, but their own. Alejandro was in middle school now, making friends, playing soccer. Isabela had lost most of her accent.

And Carlos was still in Caracas, teaching children in borrowed rooms, organizing teachers who had nothing left to lose.

"The government is cracking down again," he told her in March. His voice sounded different—tired in a way she hadn't heard before. "They arrested Ramón last week."

"Ramón from the union?"

"Yes."

"Carlos, you have to be careful."

"I'm always careful."

But careful didn't mean safe. Careful didn't mean anything in a country where people disappeared for saying the wrong thing, for knowing the wrong person, for being in the wrong place.

"I worry about you," she said. "Every day, I worry."

"I know." A pause. "I worry about you too. About the kids. Whether I made the right choice, letting you go."

Letting her go. As if she had asked permission. As if he had given it.

"We're okay," she said. "We're safe."

"I know. That's the only thing that makes any of this bearable."

On a Saturday afternoon, Elena sat in the living room helping Isabela with homework while Alejandro played a video game in the corner. The apartment was quiet except for the beeping of the game and the scratch of Isabela's pencil.

"Mami," Isabela said, not looking up from her worksheet. "When is Papi coming?"

Elena's hand stilled on the page. "I don't know, *mi amor.*"

"Sofia's dad lives with them. Why doesn't Papi live with us?"

"Papi has important work in Venezuela. He's helping people there."

"But we're here." Isabela looked up, her dark eyes—Carlos's eyes—searching Elena's face. "Doesn't he want to help us?"

Elena pulled her daughter close, breathing in the smell of her hair, the strawberry shampoo she insisted on using. "He loves you so much, Isabela. More than anything in the world. Sometimes loving someone means being far away from them for a while."

"That doesn't make sense."

"I know, *corazón*. I know it doesn't."

From the corner, Alejandro's game beeped and crashed. He didn't react, just sat staring at the screen. Elena wondered how much he had heard. He was twelve now—old enough to understand more than he let on, old enough to have his own questions he never asked.

She thought about Carlos in that empty apartment, teaching by candlelight, waiting for a knock on the door that might be a student or might be something worse. She thought about the life they had planned together, the future that had seemed so clear when they were young and Caracas was still a city where you could dream.

She had made the right choice. She had to believe that. But the right choice and the easy choice were not the same thing, and some nights the distance between Atlanta and Caracas felt like a wound that would never heal.

The call came on a Thursday evening, earlier than usual.

"Elena." Carlos's voice was strange—too bright, almost manic. "I have news."

Her heart seized. "What happened?"

"I got a visa. A colleague at the university, she has connections, she helped me apply—Elena, I got a visa."

For a moment she couldn't speak. "You're coming?"

"I'm coming. Three weeks. I'll be there in three weeks."

She sat down hard on the edge of the bed, her legs suddenly unable to hold her. "Carlos—"

"I know. I know I said I wouldn't leave. I know I said I had to stay and fight. But they came to the school yesterday, Elena. They took the list of names. My name was on it."

"Oh God."

"I'm okay. I wasn't there. But I can't go back. I can't—" His voice broke. "I was so stupid. I was so sure I was doing the right thing, and now I have nothing. The school is gone. The union is gone. Everyone is scattered or arrested or—"

"You're coming here," Elena said. "That's what matters. You're coming here."

"I'm sorry," he said. "I'm sorry I made you do this alone. I'm sorry I wasn't—"

"Don't. Not now. We can talk about everything when you're here."

"Three weeks."

"Three weeks."

When she hung up, she sat in the dark for a long time, the same way she had sat after so many other calls. But this time the silence felt different. Not empty. Full of something she had almost forgotten how to feel.

She would have to tell the children. She would have to figure out where he would sleep, how they would manage, what came next. There were a thousand questions and no answers yet.

But he was coming. After everything—the arguments, the distance, the silence that had grown between them like scar tissue—he was coming.

In the morning, she would tell the children. She would watch Isabela's face light up, watch Alejandro pretend he didn't care as much as he did. She would answer their questions—*when, how long, where will he sleep*—and she would not have answers for the harder ones. Why he stayed so long. Why it took this. Whether the father who arrived would be the father they remembered.

Three weeks.

She turned off the light and lay down in the dark, listening to the city outside, waiting for a sleep that wouldn't come.

11. Rosa

It's Mother's Day, and Rosa Alvarez is sitting in a migrant shelter in Nogales, Mexico, holding a photograph of her children.

Mauricio is twelve in the picture, though he's thirteen now—she missed his birthday. Lupe is nine, Carla seven. They're standing in front of the house in Philadelphia, the little brick row house she and Javier bought six years ago, the one with the cracked front step they kept meaning to fix. In the photo, the children are smiling. Mauricio has his arms around his sisters, protective, the way he's been since he was old enough to walk.

She traces their faces with her thumb, the way she does every morning, the way she's done for four months now. Four months since she left them. Four months since she walked out of that house and got on a bus heading south, knowing she might never walk back in.

Her phone buzzes. Javier.

She steps outside the shelter into the morning heat and answers.

"*Bueno.*"

"Rosa." His voice is flat, tired. It's 7 a.m. in Philadelphia—he must be getting the kids ready for school. "The girls wanted to talk to you. It's Mother's Day."

"I know." She closes her eyes. "Put them on."

A shuffle, then Carla's voice, high and bright: "Mami! Happy Mother's Day! We made you a card but we can't send it because you're not here."

"I know, *mi amor*. Tell me about the card."

"It has flowers. And a heart. Lupe drew the heart but I did the flowers. When are you coming home?"

The question she can't answer. "Soon, *corazón*. I hope soon."

"You said that last time."

"I know."

More shuffling. Lupe's voice now, quieter: "Hi, Mami."

"Hi, *mija*. How are you?"

"Fine." A pause. "Papi burned the eggs again."

Rosa almost laughs. "He never could cook."

"I miss you."

"I miss you too. So much. More than I can say."

"Mami?" Lupe's voice drops to a whisper. "Mauricio says you're not coming back. He says you left us like Tía Berta left her kids. Is that true?"

Rosa's throat tightens. "No, *mija*. That's not true. I didn't leave you. I'm trying to come back. I'm trying so hard."

"Then why can't you?"

Before she can answer, there's a clatter—the phone being taken. Then Mauricio's voice, hard in a way that makes her stomach clench.

"The bus is here. We have to go."

"Mauricio, *mijo*—"

"Bye."

The line goes dead.

Rosa stands in the dusty street outside the shelter, the phone still pressed to her ear, listening to nothing.

She came to see her mother die. That's the simple version. The version she tells the other women in the shelter, the version that makes sense.

The longer version: Her father died eight years ago, cancer that ate through him in six months, and Rosa was in Philadelphia scrubbing office floors at night and couldn't go. Couldn't risk it. Javier had just lost his job, the kids were small, and if she left and couldn't get back, what would happen to them?

So she sent money. She called every day. She listened to her mother cry on the phone, and she told herself it was the right choice, and when her father died she wasn't there to hold his hand, wasn't there to say goodbye, wasn't there to put a flower on his coffin. Her brother in Montana—also undocumented— couldn't go either. Their father was buried by neighbors.

She swore she would never let that happen again.

When her mother got sick—the same cancer, as if the disease ran in the family like eye color or the shape of a nose— Rosa knew what she had to do. She knew the risk. She'd been in the US for twenty-three years without papers, and if she left, the law said she couldn't come back for ten years. The ten-year bar, they call it. Doesn't matter that her children are American citizens. Doesn't matter that her whole life is there. She was illegal, she left, and now the door is locked behind her.

But her mother was dying. And Rosa had already missed one parent's death. She couldn't miss another.

"Go," Javier said, the night she told him. He was sitting at the kitchen table, his hands wrapped around a cup of coffee that had gone cold. "You have to go. We'll figure it out."

"What if I can't get back?"

He looked at her, and she saw the fear in his eyes, the same fear that was twisting in her own chest. "Then we'll figure that out too."

She was with her mother for three weeks. She held her hand through the pain, changed her sheets, spooned broth into her mouth when she could still swallow. At the end, her mother's eyes opened one last time, focused on Rosa's face.

"*Mija,*" she whispered. "*Gracias a Dios.* You came."

"I came, Mamá."

"*Te quiero.*"

"*Te quiero, Mamá.*"

Her mother closed her eyes and didn't open them again.

The first time Rosa tried to cross back, she made it three miles into the desert before the Border Patrol found her.

They put her on a bus to Nogales, and she walked into this same shelter, and she waited a week, and she tried again.

The second time was worse.

She was with a group of eight—four men, three other women, a teenager who couldn't have been older than sixteen. The coyote led them through the desert at night, following paths he said he knew. On the third night, they saw the lights.

"*La migra*," someone hissed, and they scattered.

Rosa ran. She doesn't know for how long—minutes, maybe, or hours. The desert was black except for the stars, and she couldn't see her feet, couldn't see the rocks and brush that tore at her legs. When the flashlight hit her face, she stopped. There was nowhere left to go.

They put her in a van. Then a cell.

The detention center was cold in a way she hadn't known buildings could be cold. The lights stayed on twenty-four hours a day—fluorescent white, humming and flickering, making it impossible to know if it was morning or night. They gave her a thin mat to sleep on, a blanket that smelled like disinfectant. The other women in the cell were strangers. They didn't talk much. What was there to say?

Thirty days.

She counted them on the wall with a fingernail, tiny scratches no one else could see. She thought about her children every minute of every day. She thought about Mauricio's face when she left, the way he'd hugged her too hard and then pulled away, embarrassed by his own need. She thought about Carla asking if she could come with her, and Rosa saying no, *mija*, you have school, not telling her the truth: that the journey was too dangerous, that she might not make it, that she couldn't risk her daughter's life along with her own.

When they released her, they put her on another bus back to Nogales.

"Next time," the agent said, not unkindly, "it's ninety days. And another felony charge. You understand?"

She understood.

Ninety days. Three months in that cold, bright cell.

And even if she survives that, even if she tries again and again, there's the ten-year bar. She is legally prohibited from entering the United States for ten years from the day she left. Her children will be twenty-three, nineteen, and seventeen by the time that window opens. They will have grown up without her.

People ask why she doesn't just apply for a visa. Her children are citizens, after all. Surely that counts for something.

It doesn't. Or rather, it does—but only after the ten years have passed. The law doesn't care that her children need their mother now. The law doesn't care that Carla still cries at night, that Lupe has started wetting the bed, that Mauricio has stopped talking to anyone about anything. The law only cares that Rosa was in the country illegally for twenty-three years, and when she left, she triggered a punishment designed to keep families apart.

She knows the statistics. She's heard them from the lawyers who sometimes visit the shelter, offering free consultations that always end the same way: *I'm sorry, there's nothing we can do.* Millions of people are caught in this trap—parents separated from citizen children, husbands from wives, families split by a

law that pretends to protect the border but really just destroys
lives.

"It's not about keeping people out," one lawyer told her.
"It's about punishing people for being here. For building lives.
For having children who belong."

Javier calls less often now.

At first it was every day, sometimes twice. They would talk
until the phone credit ran out, saying nothing and everything,
just needing to hear each other's voices. But the calls have
gotten shorter. The silences have gotten longer.

Last week, he said: "Rosa, I don't know how much longer I
can do this."

"I know."

"The kids need things I can't give them. Carla had a
nightmare and she wanted you. I didn't know what to do."

"Tell her I love her. Tell her I'm coming."

"I've been telling her that for four months."

Rosa didn't answer. What could she say?

"There's a woman at work," Javier said, and Rosa's blood
went cold. "She's been helping with the kids sometimes. Picking
them up when I have to stay late."

"Javier—"

"Nothing's happened. I swear to you, nothing's happened.
But Rosa..." His voice broke. "I'm so tired. I'm so goddamn
tired."

"I know," she said. "I know you are."

When they hung up, she sat outside the shelter and watched the sun set over the border wall, and she thought about the woman at Javier's work, and she thought about her children calling someone else *Mami*, and she thought about the ten years stretching ahead of her like a desert she would never cross.

There are three options.

She can try to cross again. Risk ninety days in detention, another felony charge, her name in a system that will follow her forever. Risk dying in the desert like so many others—becoming one of those anonymous crosses stuck in the sand, no name, no date, a mother who disappeared and never came home.

She can stay in Mexico. Wait out the ten-year bar in a country she left when she was seventeen, where she has no job, no family, no home. Wait for her children to grow up without her, hoping they'll still know her face when she's finally allowed to return.

Or she can give up. Accept that the life she built is gone. Accept that her children will be raised by their father and maybe by the woman from his work. Accept that she made a choice— to see her mother die—and this is the price.

None of these is a choice. All of them are.

The other women in the shelter have started to notice that Rosa is different today. She moves with more purpose. She packed her small bag this morning, the one with the photograph and the rosary and the single change of clothes. She said goodbye to Liliana, who arrived last month from Honduras, and to Manuela, who has been here longer than anyone and knows everyone's story.

"You've decided," Manuela said. It wasn't a question.

"Yes."

"Are you going to tell me what?"

Rosa looked at her—this woman who had held so many other women in this same doorway, who had seen them leave and sometimes seen them come back and sometimes never seen them again.

"No," Rosa said. "I don't think I am."

Manuela nodded slowly. Then she pulled Rosa into a hug, the kind of hug Rosa's mother used to give, the kind that says everything without words.

"*Que Dios te bendiga, mija,*" Manuela whispered. "Whatever you choose."

Rosa steps out of the shelter into the bright Nogales morning. The sun is already hot, the sky a hard blue, the border wall visible in the distance like a scar across the earth.

She doesn't know if she's walking toward her children or away from them. She doesn't know if the choice she's made is brave or foolish, an act of love or an act of surrender.

She only knows that she's made it.

She starts walking.

12. Karina

The girl's name is Yesenia. She's nineteen, from Honduras, and she arrived at the shelter three hours ago with nothing but a plastic bag and a bruise on her cheekbone that's already turning yellow at the edges. She hasn't spoken since she got here. She sits on the cot in the corner, her knees pulled to her chest, her eyes fixed on something no one else can see.

Karina knows that look. She wore it herself, once.

She doesn't go to Yesenia right away. She waits. She folds towels, organizes the donation bins, helps Estela prepare the evening meal. But she keeps the girl in her peripheral vision, watches for the moment when the silence becomes unbearable.

It comes around six o'clock. Yesenia's shoulders start to shake—no sound, just trembling. Karina sets down the stack of sheets she's carrying and walks over. She doesn't say anything. She just sits on the cot beside her, leaving space between them, and waits.

After a long time, Yesenia whispers: "How do you do it?"

Karina doesn't pretend not to understand. "Some days I don't. Some days I can't get out of bed. But I get up anyway."

"Why?"

"Because someone sat with me once, when I couldn't speak. And it helped."

Yesenia is quiet. Then, so softly Karina almost doesn't hear: "Will it always feel like this?"

Karina considers lying. She doesn't.

"Some of it gets easier. Some of it doesn't. You learn to carry it differently. That's all I can promise you."

This is what I can tell you about Karina Rivas:

She is thirty-four years old. She is from El Chorrillo, a neighborhood in Panama City that most Americans have never heard of, though American bombs fell there in 1989, before she was born. She was studying to be a teacher when she met the man who would become her husband. She was twenty-one and believed in things like fairy tales and fresh starts.

She doesn't believe in fairy tales anymore.

When I ask if I can interview her for this book, she studies me for a long moment—measuring, assessing. Then she nods.

"Estela says you're not like the others," she says. "She says you listen."

"I try."

"Good." She sits down across from me, her back straight, her hands folded on the table. "Because I'm only going to tell this once. And there are parts I won't tell at all."

"Miguel was charming," Karina says. "That's what everyone remembers. The flowers, the notes, the way he'd look at you like you were the only person in the room. By the time I understood what he really was, I was already his wife."

The escalation was gradual. First the comments about her clothes—*Ese vestido es demasiado provocativo, mi amor*—then about

110

her friends, her family, her time. Then the first slap, and the tears afterward, and the promises. Then more.

"In our community, you don't leave your husband," Karina says. "My own mother told me: *La cruz que Dios te da, es la que tienes que cargar.* The cross God gives you is the one you must bear."

She pauses. "I told her he was beating me. She said to pray more."

I ask about the isolation—how it happened, how complete it became.

"Miguel was a politician. Everyone loved him. He ran charity events, helped families, gave speeches about community values." Her voice goes flat. "When I finally showed my best friend the bruises, she said I must be mistaken. She said maybe if I tried harder to please him, things would be different."

"And the police?"

"I called them once. After he broke my rib." Karina's jaw tightens. "They came, they saw him standing there in his nice suit, and they asked if he needed help controlling his *hysterical* wife."

She doesn't describe the night she left in detail. She gives me the bones: their anniversary, his rage, the certainty that he would kill her this time. The moment when something inside her snapped.

"He passed out drunk. I took my passport, some money I'd been hiding, and I called my cousin Ari." Karina's hands, which have been still until now, begin to move—folding and unfolding a napkin, as if they need something to do. "Ari had left an abusive marriage years before. She understood. She didn't ask questions. She just said, *I'll make some calls.*"

"And the journey north?"

Karina is quiet for a moment. Then: "The first group Ari connected me with was legitimate. They helped women like me. But after the first leg, I was passed to another group. And then another." She looks at me directly. "Do you know what it's like to be cargo? To be handed off like a package, each time to men who are worse than the last?"

I shake my head.

"Good," she says. "I hope you never do."

There are parts she won't tell me. She makes this clear with a single sentence: "Something happened in the desert that I don't talk about. Not to anyone." She doesn't elaborate. She doesn't need to. The shape of her silence tells me everything.

What she does describe: the heat in the back of the truck. The stench of sweat and fear. The way the other migrants looked away when one of the smugglers pulled her aside. The hollowness that followed.

"I kept asking myself: *Is this the price of freedom?*" She shakes her head. "I had escaped one hell and found another."

At the border, everything happened fast. The ICE agents appeared out of nowhere. The smuggler who had hurt her melted into the group, pretending to be just another migrant. Karina was too terrified to say anything.

Then, in detention—a place she describes as overcrowded and reeking of despair—something unexpected happened.

"One of the women in our group, someone I'd never even spoken to, pulled an agent aside. I saw her pointing at him. Talking fast." Karina's voice changes, softens. "I don't know her name. I never will. But she saved my life."

A female agent approached Karina privately. Asked gentle questions. Listened.

"At first I denied everything. I was too afraid." Karina looks down at her hands. "But she waited. She didn't push. And finally I just... broke. Everything came out. The abuse in Panama, the journey, what happened in the desert."

The agent believed her. A counselor was called. For the first time since leaving Panama, Karina felt like a person instead of a problem to be processed.

"They told me the assault had happened on U.S. soil," she says. "That meant they could prosecute. That meant I had rights."

What followed was not rescue. It was bureaucracy.

Karina describes a parade of interviews, evaluations, and appointments that stretched over months. Immigration lawyers, asylum officers, psychologists, law enforcement—each one requiring her to tell her story from the beginning, to relive every detail.

"Once, I spent four hours explaining everything to an asylum officer. At the end, she told me they'd lost my file. I'd have to come back and do it again." Karina's voice is steady, but her hands have stopped moving. They're gripping the edge of the table. "Another official asked why I didn't have *proof* of the abuse. As if I should have stopped to take photographs while my husband was breaking my bones."

The constant retelling took its toll. "Every time I recounted what happened, it was like reopening a wound. I'd leave those interviews feeling raw. Exposed. Sometimes I couldn't sleep for days."

But there were also lifelines. A therapist who helped her understand that telling her story wasn't just bureaucratic ritual— it was a way of reclaiming it. A support group where other women understood without needing explanations.

"We celebrated small things," Karina says. "A night without nightmares. A good interview. Someone's visa coming through." She pauses. "It was in that group that I first started to see myself as something other than what had been done to me."

The first time she spoke publicly, she almost didn't.

"I was standing backstage at a small event, and my heart was pounding so hard I thought I would die. I kept thinking: *What if they don't believe me? What if he finds out?*" Her voice drops. "For years, my survival had depended on being invisible. Standing up and speaking was like painting a target on my back."

She did it anyway. Afterward, she went home and curled up in bed, shaking, unable to eat or sleep.

"I felt like I was held together with tape and glue," she says. "Every time I told my story, it was like peeling off another layer of that tape. Exposing the cracks underneath."

But then something changed. After one event, a young woman approached her in tears.

"She said that hearing me had given her the courage to leave her own situation." Karina's voice catches, just for a moment. "That was when I understood. My pain could have a purpose. My voice could matter."

I ask her what healing looks like.

She laughs—short, bitter. "People want a redemption story. They want me to say I'm whole now, that I've moved past it. I can't give them that."

She meets my eyes. "There are still nights when I wake up screaming. There are still sounds that make me flinch—a raised voice, a door slamming. There are still days when I can't leave my apartment."

"Then why do you keep doing this work?"

"Because someone has to." She gestures toward the main room of the shelter, where Yesenia is now sitting with Estela, eating soup. "Because that girl needs to know she's not alone. Because I remember what it was like to think no one would ever believe me."

She pauses. "And because every woman I help is another piece of myself I get back. Not the pieces that were taken— those are gone. But new ones. Different ones."

I ask what she wants people to understand.

"That we're not numbers. Not cases." Her voice hardens. "That the system that's supposed to help us often breaks us instead. That healing isn't a straight line, and it doesn't have an ending. You don't *get over* this. You learn to live with it."

She looks toward the window, toward the fading light.

"And that choosing to be visible, after years of hiding, is the hardest thing I've ever done. Harder than leaving Miguel. Harder than the journey. Because every time I speak, I'm choosing to be seen. And some part of me is still terrified that being seen will get me killed."

"But you do it anyway."

"I do it anyway."

Later that evening, I watch Karina from across the room. A new woman has arrived at the shelter—older, maybe fifty, with gray in her hair and a haunted look in her eyes. She sits alone on a cot, clutching a rosary.

Karina notices. She sets down what she's doing. She walks over, slowly, giving the woman time to see her coming.

She sits down beside her. Leaves space between them.

And waits.

13. Javier

The morgue is cold in a way that feels intentional, as if the temperature itself is meant to prepare you. Ana follows the attendant down a corridor of white walls and fluorescent light, her footsteps echoing against tile. She has flown from Puebla to Seattle, then driven to Tacoma, then waited in a government office for three hours while someone found the right form. Now she is here.

The attendant stops at a door. "Take as long as you need," he says, and she can tell he has said this many times before.

The room is small. A steel table. A white sheet over a shape she has known her whole life.

Ana pulls back the sheet.

Javier's face is wrong—the color drained, the stillness absolute. His eyes are closed. She touches his cheek and it is cold, and she understands in her body what she has known in her mind for six days: her brother is dead, and no one will tell her why.

The phone call came on a Tuesday, early morning. An unfamiliar number.

"Are you the sister of Javier Morales?"

"Yes."

"This is Officer Rivera with Immigration and Customs Enforcement. I'm calling to inform you that your brother passed away in custody on Saturday evening. We're sorry for your loss."

Ana remembers asking questions. She remembers the answers being short, rehearsed, empty. *Cause of death is under investigation. We can't release details at this time. Someone will be in touch about next steps.*

She remembers screaming after she hung up.

What Ana knows, in the beginning, fits on a single page:

Javier Morales, 34. Detained by ICE on March 15th, outside the hospital in Hastings, Nebraska, where he had been treated for a workplace injury. Transferred to the Northwest Detention Center in Tacoma, Washington. Died in custody on September 3rd. Cause of death: undetermined.

Undetermined. Six months in their custody, and they cannot say how he died.

Ana begins to make calls.

The Northwest Detention Center does not return her messages. The ICE public affairs office sends her a form letter expressing condolences. The Mexican consulate is sympathetic but can offer little beyond assistance with paperwork.

She files a Freedom of Information Act request. She contacts immigrant rights organizations in Seattle and Tacoma. She finds a lawyer who agrees to help pro bono, a woman named Margaret Chen who has handled cases like this before.

"Cases like this," Margaret says carefully, when they first speak, "are difficult. The detention system is designed to be opaque. Records go missing. Timelines don't match. And they know that most families don't have the resources to push back."

"I'll push back," Ana says.

The documents arrive in pieces, over weeks.

First: Javier's intake forms. Medical history marked "unremarkable," despite the fact that he had been hospitalized for a severe hand laceration less than forty-eight hours before his arrest. The injury is not mentioned.

Second: commissary records. Javier bought stamps. Envelopes. A small English-Spanish dictionary. The records stop in June.

Third: medical request forms. Seven of them, filed between April and August.

April 12: *Request for follow-up care, hand injury. Status: Pending.*

April 29: *Request for pain medication. Status: Denied—see facility physician.*

May 15: *Request to see facility physician. Status: Pending.*

June 3: *Request for mental health evaluation. Status: Pending.*

The last three requests, filed in July and August, are identical: *Request for medical attention. Urgent.* All three are marked *Pending.*

Ana stares at the word. *Pending.* As if he were still waiting.

She learns about the meatpacking plant from a man named Tomás, who worked alongside Javier in Hastings.

"He was a good guy," Tomás says. They are speaking by phone; he is still in Nebraska, still working. "Shared his food. Always had a joke, even when things were bad." He pauses. "He had a picture of his niece in his locker. Talked about her all the time. Said he was saving up to go back for her quinceañera."

"Lucía," Ana says. "My daughter."

"Yeah. Lucía." Tomás is quiet for a moment. "The day he got hurt, the supervisor didn't even stop the line. Just told them to get him out of there and clean up the blood. I helped carry him to the truck."

"And then?"

"And then we went back to work. They docked us for the time."

What Ana learns about the accident:

The machinery was faulty. The supervisor knew. He ordered them to fix it without stopping production. Javier slipped on the blood-slicked floor—there was always blood on the floor—and his hand came down on a jagged edge of metal.

At the hospital, he was alone. His coworkers had been ordered back to the plant. His employer never called, never visited, never offered to help with the bills.

Two days later, still bandaged, still weak, Javier was arrested in the hospital parking lot. An ICE officer had been tipped off—Ana never learns by whom.

The hardest document to obtain is the incident report from July 19th, the day Javier was transferred to solitary confinement.

When it finally arrives, most of it is redacted. Black bars cover the narrative section, the witness statements, the justification for transfer. What remains: Javier's name, his detainee number, the date, and a single phrase visible through the ink: *non-compliance with facility directives.*

Ana calls Margaret. "What does that mean? Non-compliance?"

"It could mean anything. Talking back. Asking too many questions. Filing too many medical requests." Margaret's voice is flat. "They don't need a real reason. And they don't have to tell you what it was."

There is one person who can tell Ana what happened in solitary, and it takes her three months to find him.

His name is Eduardo. He was detained at the Northwest Detention Center from May through October, in the cell next to Javier's. He has since been deported to Guatemala, but Ana tracks him down through a network of advocacy organizations, and they speak by phone on a crackling connection.

"I could hear him through the wall," Eduardo says. His voice is steady, but Ana can hear the effort it takes. "At first, he would talk. To himself, I think. Or maybe to God. I couldn't make out the words, but I could hear his voice."

"And then?"

"And then he stopped talking. For a while, I heard him pacing. Back and forth, back and forth. The cells were small—four steps one way, four steps back. I counted."

Eduardo pauses.

"Then he started calling out. Asking for help. Saying his hand was infected, saying he needed a doctor. The guards would walk by and he'd call to them. They didn't answer."

Ana is writing this down, her hand shaking.

"How long?"

"Weeks. Maybe a month. I lost track of time in there—you do that. But I remember the day it got quiet. I knocked on the wall and he didn't knock back." Eduardo's voice breaks. "I didn't hear anything after that. A few days later, they took him out. I didn't know he was dead until someone told me later."

The death certificate arrives last.

Cause of death: *Undetermined.*

Manner of death: *Pending investigation.*

There will be no investigation. Ana knows this now. Margaret has explained how it works: an internal review, conducted by ICE, which will conclude that all protocols were followed. No one will be disciplined. No one will be named. The file will be closed.

Ana sits at her kitchen table in Puebla, the documents spread before her. Seven medical requests, all pending. An incident report, mostly redacted. Commissary records showing her brother bought stamps and envelopes—letters he must have written, letters she never received. A death certificate that says nothing.

She knows how he was hurt. She knows he asked for help and was ignored. She knows he spent his final weeks in a cell the size of a closet, calling out to guards who walked past without answering.

She does not know his last words. She does not know if he was conscious at the end, or if he was alone, or if anyone held his hand. She does not know what he was thinking when he understood that no one was coming.

She will never know.

***

Javier's body is returned to Mexico in October, after weeks of paperwork and fees and phone calls to offices that kept losing his file.

At the funeral, Ana does not speak. Her mother speaks, and then an uncle, and then a priest who did not know Javier but says the right things about God's mercy and the mystery of suffering.

Ana stands at the grave with Lucía, who is twelve now, who will not have a quinceañera with her uncle there, who keeps asking questions that Ana cannot answer.

Why did he go? Why didn't he come back? Why didn't anyone help him?

***

Later—weeks later, months later—Ana will give interviews. She will speak at rallies and press conferences. She will file a wrongful death lawsuit that will be dismissed, and then appeal it, and then settle for an amount that the detention company's lawyers will describe as "not an admission of liability."

She will become, in the language of the movement, an advocate. A voice for the voiceless. A symbol of something larger than herself.

But that is later.

For now, she sits at her kitchen table, the documents spread before her. Outside, it is evening. Lucía is doing homework in the next room. The house is quiet.

Ana looks at the medical request forms. Seven of them. *Pending. Pending. Pending.*

She thinks about the word. Thinks about her brother in a cell the size of a closet, waiting for someone to answer.

No one answered.

She gathers the documents into a folder, puts the folder in a drawer, and closes it.

The evidence is all there. The evidence will never be enough.

14. Rodrigo

The alarm goes off at 5:30, same as every morning. Rodrigo reaches over to silence it before it wakes Kathleen, but she's already stirring, her hand finding his arm in the dark.

"You're up," she murmurs.

"Go back to sleep."

She does. He watches her for a moment—the way her hair falls across the pillow, the slight furrow between her brows even in sleep—and then he eases out of bed and pads down the hallway in his socks.

The house is quiet. Sofia's door is closed; she's fourteen now and sleeps until the last possible minute. Miguel, eleven, is sprawled sideways across his bed, one foot hanging off the edge. Ana, the youngest at eight, has kicked off her covers again. Rodrigo pulls the blanket back over her, and she doesn't stir.

Downstairs, he makes coffee. Stands at the kitchen window while it brews, looking out at the backyard—the fence he built last summer, the swing set the kids have mostly outgrown but Ana still uses, the grass that needs mowing. Beyond the fence, the first light is touching the hills east of Wenatchee.

Twenty-two years. He's been in this country twenty-two years now. More than half his life.

He thinks about this sometimes, when the house is quiet and everyone else is asleep. He came here with nothing—a backpack, a few dollars, a seventeen-year-old's certainty that things had to be better somewhere else. And now there's this:

the house, the kids, Kathleen. The truck in the driveway with MENJIVAR CONSTRUCTION on the side. The coffee maker that cost too much but Kathleen wanted it, so he bought it.

A life. His life.

He drinks his coffee, eats toast standing at the counter, leaves a note for Kathleen: *Job site until 5. Sofia has practice—can you pick her up? Love you.*

At 6:15, he's in the truck, heading toward the new development on the north side of town. The radio plays a song he doesn't know. The sun comes up over the orchards, and Rodrigo drives to work.

The traffic stop happens on a Tuesday evening in July.

Rodrigo is driving home from the job site, windows down, thinking about dinner. Kathleen said something about pasta. Or maybe that was yesterday. He's trying to remember when he sees the lights in his rearview mirror—red and blue, pulsing.

He pulls over. His heart is beating faster than it should be, but he tells himself it's nothing. A taillight, maybe. Registration. Something fixable.

The officer approaches. Young, white, hand resting on his belt.

"License and registration."

Rodrigo hands them over. His hands are steady.

"You know your left taillight is out?"

"No, sir. I'll get it fixed."

The officer looks at the license. Looks at Rodrigo. Something shifts in his expression.

"Where are you from, Mr. Menjivar?"

Rodrigo feels the ground tilt beneath him. Twenty-two years of dreading this question.

"El Salvador, originally. But I've lived here—"

"Wait here."

The officer walks back to his cruiser. Rodrigo watches in the mirror. The officer is on the radio now, talking to someone. The minutes stretch. Five, ten. The sun is setting, turning the sky orange and pink, and Rodrigo thinks about Sofia at soccer practice, about Kathleen starting dinner, about the life that is happening right now without him, just a few miles away.

When the officer returns, his face has changed.

"Step out of the vehicle, Mr. Menjivar."

"Officer, please—I have a family—"

"Out of the vehicle. Now."

The lawyer's office is small and cluttered, files stacked on every surface. Kathleen sits across the desk, her hands clenched in her lap.

"I'm sorry, Mrs. Menjivar." The lawyer's voice is gentle, which makes it worse. "Because your husband entered the country without documentation and never adjusted his status, our options are extremely limited."

"But we're married. We have three children. American citizens. Doesn't that count for anything?"

"It should." The lawyer pauses. "But under current law, it's not enough. If he'd applied for adjustment of status years ago—"

"We meant to. We always meant to." Kathleen's voice cracks. "There was always something else. The kids, the business, the—" She stops. "We thought we had time."

The lawyer doesn't say anything. There's nothing to say.

"So what happens now?"

"He'll be deported. Probably within the week. There's an expedited process—"

"A week?"

"I'm sorry."

Kathleen drives home in silence. The kids are at her mother's. The house is empty. She stands in the kitchen, looking at Rodrigo's note from that morning, still on the counter. *Love you.*

She doesn't cry. Not yet. There will be time for that later, she thinks. Years of time.

The plane lands in San Salvador at 11:47 in the morning.

Rodrigo walks down the jetway in the clothes he was arrested in—work jeans, a T-shirt with a small hole near the hem, boots that still have Washington dust on them. He has forty-three dollars in his pocket and a phone number for his grandmother, written on a scrap of paper.

At the immigration desk, a bored official stamps his papers without looking up.

"*Bienvenido a El Salvador, Señor Menjivar.*"

Welcome back.

Rodrigo wants to say something—that this isn't back, that back is 2,800 miles north, in a house with a fence he built and children who are wondering where he is. Instead, he takes his papers and walks out into the heat.

San Salvador is loud, bright, chaotic. The streets are clogged with traffic; vendors shout from the sidewalks; music blares from open windows. Rodrigo recognizes none of it. He left this city when he was seventeen, and the seventeen-year-old who left is a stranger to him now.

He takes a bus to Mejicanos, to the neighborhood where his grandmother still lives. The trip takes two hours. He watches the city give way to crowded suburbs, graffiti-covered walls, clusters of young men on corners who watch the bus pass with flat, assessing eyes.

His grandmother is waiting at the door.

"*Ay, mijo.*" She pulls him inside, her embrace fierce despite her frailness. "You shouldn't have come."

"I didn't have a choice, Abuela."

"I know." She glances at the window, at the street beyond. "But it's not safe here. The *maras*—they control everything now. And you—" She touches his arm, where SOFIA is tattooed in simple script. "They'll think this means something. They'll think you're from the other side."

"It's my daughter's name."

"They won't ask."

That night, Rodrigo lies on a thin mattress in the room where he slept as a child. The walls are the same pale blue. The window is the same, looking out on the same narrow street. But everything else has changed.

He can hear gunshots in the distance. Dogs barking. A car with no muffler. He thinks about Sofia, about Miguel, about Ana. He thinks about Kathleen, alone in their bed. He thinks about the fence, the swing set, the coffee maker.

He does not sleep.

On the second day, they find him.

He's walking back from the tienda, a bag of rice in his hand, when three young men step into his path. Teenagers, maybe. Hard to tell. Their faces are older than their years.

"*Oye, gringo.*" The one in front grins, but his eyes are empty. "*¿Estás perdido?*"

"No. Just going home."

The young man's gaze drops to Rodrigo's arm. The tattoo.

"Nice ink." He reaches out, grabs Rodrigo's wrist, twists it to see better. "What's this? Sofia?" He pronounces it wrong—*So-FEE-ah*, like it's a gang name. "You 18th Street? You come here to start something?"

"It's my daughter. I have a daughter named Sofia. In Washington. In the United States."

The young man laughs. The others join in.

"Sure, *gringo*. Your daughter." He releases Rodrigo's wrist, shoves him backward. "We'll be seeing you."

Rodrigo walks home fast, his heart pounding. His grandmother is at the window when he arrives, her face tight with fear.

"They spoke to you."

"Yes."

"You have to leave. Tonight. Go somewhere else—another city, another country. You can't stay here."

"Where would I go?"

She doesn't answer. They both know there's nowhere.

On the third morning, they come for him.

Rodrigo hears the car first—engine gunning, tires on gravel. Then the pounding on the door, so hard the whole house shakes.

His grandmother is already up, standing in the hallway in her nightgown, her hand pressed to her mouth.

"Don't answer it," she whispers.

But the door is already splintering. Four of them this time, older than the boys on the street, their arms sleeved in tattoos. They don't speak. They don't need to.

Two of them grab Rodrigo by the arms. He struggles, but they're stronger, and there are more of them, and he knows—he knows with a certainty that closes over him like water—that this is how it ends.

"*Abuela—*"

"*Mijo!*" She reaches for him, but one of the men shoves her back. She hits the wall, slides down it, her eyes never leaving Rodrigo's face.

They drag him out into the morning light. The street is empty. No—not empty. Rodrigo sees curtains twitch, faces appear and disappear. The neighbors are watching. No one moves to help.

The car is waiting, engine running. They push him into the back seat, and the door slams, and the car pulls away, and the last thing Rodrigo sees is his grandmother in the doorway, her hand raised, her mouth open in a scream he can no longer hear.

They find his body that afternoon, in an alley on the eastern edge of Mejicanos. A neighbor comes to tell his grandmother—a woman who has seen this before, who knows the words by heart.

The grandmother does not scream. She does not cry. She walks to the police station, files a report that she knows will go nowhere, and then she walks home and sits in the chair by the window and does not move until dark.

At 9:47 that night, Washington time, she calls Kathleen.

The phone rings three times. Kathleen is in the kitchen, cleaning up after dinner. The kids are upstairs—Sofia doing homework, Miguel on his computer, Ana already asleep.

"Hello?"

"*Señora Menjivar.*" The voice is old, cracked, speaking in Spanish. "*Soy la abuela de Rodrigo.*"

Kathleen's hand tightens on the phone. "Is he—"

The grandmother tells her. The words come slowly, carefully, as if each one costs something. When she finishes, there is silence on the line—a silence that stretches across 2,800 miles, across borders and time zones, across everything that was supposed to protect them and didn't.

Then Kathleen makes a sound. Not a scream. Something smaller, more broken. The sound of a life collapsing inward.

The house is quiet now.

It's been three weeks. The kids are at school. Kathleen is sitting at the kitchen table, not eating breakfast, not drinking the coffee that has gone cold in front of her.

Rodrigo's work boots are still by the back door. She hasn't moved them. She can't. Every time she looks at them, she thinks: *He'll need those when he comes home.* And then she remembers that he won't.

The truck is in the driveway. MENJIVAR CONSTRUCTION. The jobs have been cancelled, referred to other contractors. She'll have to sell the truck eventually. She'll have to do a lot of things eventually. But not yet.

Sofia has stopped talking. She goes to school, comes home, closes her door. Miguel has started wetting the bed again, something he hasn't done since he was six. Ana keeps asking when Daddy is coming back, and Kathleen keeps saying *soon, mija, soon,* because she doesn't have the words for the truth.

A broken taillight. That's what started it. A bulb that cost four dollars to replace.

She thinks about this constantly. If he'd checked the lights that morning. If he'd taken a different route. If the officer had been different, kinder, less suspicious. If they'd filed the paperwork years ago, when they first talked about it, when the kids were small and there was still time.

If, if, if.

The coffee is cold. The house is quiet. Outside, the sun is shining on the fence Rodrigo built, on the swing set, on the grass that still needs mowing.

Kathleen sits at the table and does not move.

His boots are by the door.

He is not coming home.

15. Alejandro

The center is quiet at 6:15 in the morning.

Alejandro unlocks the front door, disables the alarm, flips on the lights one bank at a time. The fluorescents flicker and hum. He likes this hour—the stillness before the day begins, before the waiting room fills with people who need things he may or may not be able to give them.

He starts the coffee. Checks the voicemail: seven messages overnight, three in Spanish, two in English, one in something that might be Haitian Creole, one that's just breathing and then a click. He writes down names, numbers, the few details people leave. *Mercedes, needs lawyer, deportation hearing next week. Samuel, work permit question. Someone's cousin in detention—Alejandro couldn't catch where.*

The map on his office wall has pins in it—red for Mexico and Central America, blue for South America, yellow for everywhere else. Most of the pins cluster along a crooked spine from Honduras through Guatemala into southern Mexico, then fan out across Texas. But there are outliers: a pin in Senegal, two in Haiti, one in Afghanistan, a small cluster in Venezuela. Each pin is someone who walked through the door.

Alejandro adds a pin for Silvia, who arrived yesterday. Tegucigalpa. Red.

He doesn't think about his own pin anymore—Mexico City, faded now, almost lost among the others. He was seventeen when his family crossed. He's twenty-nine now. His asylum case has been pending for twelve years.

Silvia is waiting when he opens the doors at eight.

She's sitting on the bench outside with her daughter in her lap—a girl of four, maybe five, her face pressed into her mother's shoulder. Silvia's eyes are dark-ringed, watchful. She has a plastic bag with clothes in it and a folder of documents she keeps touching, as if to make sure they're still there.

"*Buenos días*," Alejandro says. "*Soy Alejandro. ¿Silvia?*"

She nods. The girl doesn't look up.

"*Pásale. Hay café.*"

He leads them inside, gets Silvia a cup of coffee, finds crayons and paper for the girl. Lucía, her name is. She draws while her mother talks.

The story comes out in pieces: the husband who drank, who hit, who one night held a knife to her throat and told her what he would do if she ever tried to leave. The aunt in Houston who said *come, I'll help you*. The bus to the border, the three days of walking, the detention center where they took her phone and her shoelaces and put her in a room with forty other women and children.

"They let me out because of her." Silvia looks at Lucía. "The lawyer said they don't usually keep mothers with small children. But I have to go back for my hearing. In six months."

"Do you have a lawyer for the hearing?"

"The one from detention—she gave me a list of names. I've been calling." Silvia's voice flattens. "No one calls back."

Alejandro writes this down. He knows the list she means. Half the lawyers on it have waitlists of six months or more. The other half don't take cases like hers—domestic violence asylum claims are hard to win, and getting harder.

"I'm going to make some calls," he says. "There's a clinic at the law school that sometimes takes cases. And there's a lawyer named Francisco who owes me a favor."

He doesn't say: *I don't know if it will work.* He doesn't say: *The odds are not good.* He says: "We're going to figure this out. *¿Okay?*"

Silvia nods. She doesn't look like she believes him, but she nods.

The day fills up.

A man named Roberto needs help with a work permit renewal—his expires in two weeks and he filed the paperwork four months ago but never heard back. Alejandro spends forty-five minutes on hold with USCIS, then gets disconnected. He calls again.

A teenager named Diego wants to know if he can apply for DACA. Alejandro looks at his documents, does the math. Diego crossed when he was sixteen, two years too late. He aged out of eligibility by twenty-three months.

"I'm sorry," Alejandro says. He's said it so many times it should feel like nothing by now, but it doesn't.

"So what do I do?"

"You stay careful. You don't drive without a license. You don't get in trouble. And you wait."

"For what?"

"For the law to change."

Diego laughs—a short, hard sound. "That's the plan? Wait for the law to change?"

"That's the plan," Alejandro says. He doesn't say: *I've been waiting too.* He doesn't say: *My next hearing is in four months and I don't know what will happen.* He says: "I know it's not enough. I know. But it's what we have."

At lunch, Alejandro calls Francisco in Los Angeles.

They went through orientation together years ago, back when they were both new to this work. Francisco became an immigration lawyer. Alejandro became—whatever he is. Director of a community center that runs on grants and donations and volunteer hours. Someone who makes calls and fills out forms and sits with people while they wait for news that usually isn't good.

"I have a case for you," Alejandro says. "Woman from Honduras. Domestic violence. She has a daughter."

"Alejandro." Francisco's voice is tired. "I'm carrying sixty cases right now. I can't—"

"I know."

"The clinic might take it. Have you tried—"

"I'm trying everyone. You're on the list."

There's a pause. Alejandro can hear Francisco breathing, can hear the weight of it.

"Send me the file," Francisco says finally. "I'll look at it. That's all I can promise."

"That's enough. Thank you."

After he hangs up, Alejandro sits for a moment in the quiet of his office. On the wall behind him, the map bristles with pins. In his desk drawer, there's a list he doesn't look at often—names written in his own handwriting, some with dates beside them.

Marisol. Deported, 2019. Jorge. Detained, still pending. Edwin. Denied, appealed, denied again. Rodrigo.

He'd heard about Rodrigo from a lawyer in Washington State—a man who'd lived in the US for twenty-two years, deported after a traffic stop, killed by gangs three days after he landed in San Salvador. Alejandro didn't know him, but he'd known people like him. He knows what happens when the system decides you don't belong.

He closes the drawer.

———

His mother calls at three.

"*¿Ya comiste?*"

"*Sí, Mamá.*" He hasn't, but she doesn't need to know that.

"Your brother says you work too much."

"My brother works at a bank. He thinks everyone works too much."

She laughs, but there's worry in it. His mother has been worried about him since he was seventeen, since they crossed together—her and his father and his brother and him, four suitcases and nothing else. His father is gone now, heart attack six years ago. His brother got a green card through marriage, then citizenship. His mother has a visa, renewed every year, always uncertain.

Alejandro is still waiting.

"*El abogado llamó*," his mother says. "About your case. He says the hearing is confirmed. April 15."

"I know."

"He says you should be there early. He says—"

"*Mamá.* I know. I'll be there."

She's quiet for a moment. Then: "*Ten cuidado, mijo.*"

"*Siempre.*"

He hangs up and looks at the calendar on his wall. April 15. Four months. Twelve years of waiting, and in four months he'll sit in front of a judge and find out if he gets to stay.

He's helped hundreds of people prepare for that moment. He knows what to say, what documents to bring, how to dress, how to speak. He knows that none of it guarantees anything.

He goes back to work.

By six, the center is emptying out.

Silvia left hours ago with a folder full of information— phone numbers, addresses, a checklist of documents she'll need. Lucía took three of the crayons with her; Alejandro pretended not to notice. Roberto finally got through to someone at USCIS who said his permit was "in process," which means nothing but at least it's something. Diego didn't come back. Alejandro hopes he went home. He hopes he stays careful.

The volunteers have gone. The lights in the back rooms are off. Alejandro is locking the supply closet when he hears the knock.

He could pretend he didn't hear it. The center is closed. He's been here for twelve hours. His back hurts and he hasn't eaten since breakfast and there's nothing in his refrigerator at home except leftover rice and half a lime.

The knock comes again.

He walks to the front door. Through the glass, he can see a man and a boy—the man maybe thirty, the boy maybe ten. They're carrying backpacks. The man has his hand on the boy's shoulder. They look like they've been walking for a long time.

Alejandro unlocks the door.

"*Buenas noches*," the man says. His voice is hoarse. "*¿Está abierto?*"

Alejandro looks at them—the dust on their clothes, the exhaustion in their faces, the way the boy leans into his father's side. He thinks about the pins on his map, the names in his drawer, the hearing in April that might end everything or might mean nothing at all.

"*Sí*," he says, stepping back to let them in. "*Pásale. Somos Casa Esperanza.*"

He turns the lights back on.

He starts the coffee again.

Tomorrow there will be more. There are always more. And he will be here, in this room, doing what he can with what he has—not because it's enough, but because it's what there is.

The man sits down. The boy sits beside him. Alejandro pulls up a chair.

"*Cuéntame*," he says. "*Tell me.*"

And the man begins.

Epilogue

The last interview I did for this book was with a woman named Marta.

That's not her real name. None of the names in this book are real. But Marta was real—is real—somewhere in California, living a life I know almost nothing about anymore.

We met at a taqueria near her apartment. She'd agreed to talk because a friend of a friend had vouched for me. She was suspicious, which I understood. She'd learned to be careful about who she trusted with her story.

For two hours, she told me about growing up in Guatemala, about the violence that drove her family north, about the years she spent working in the shadows—cleaning houses, picking strawberries, caring for other people's children. She told me about her daughter, born here, a citizen, now in middle school and embarrassed by her mother's accent.

"She doesn't want to speak Spanish anymore," Marta said. "She says it makes her different."

Near the end, I asked what she wanted people to understand. She thought about it for a long time.

"That we're not what they say we are. That we're just people trying to live."

She looked down at her hands.

"But I don't think they want to understand. I think it's easier not to."

I didn't have anything to say to that. I still don't.

After Marta, I stopped conducting interviews. Not because I'd heard enough, but because I'd heard so much that I didn't know how to hold it all. The weight of it—the accumulation of so many lives, so many struggles, so much loss and love and stubborn hope—had become something I carried with me.

Writing these stories was my way of putting some of that weight down. Not to get rid of it, but to share it. To say: *here. Look at this. See these people.*

I don't know what happens next. I don't know if these stories will change anything—any policy, any mind, any heart. I wrote them because they deserved to be written. Because the people who trusted me with their experiences deserved to have those experiences preserved, even in fictionalized form.

The fifteen characters in this book are composites. But the loneliness is real. The fear is real. The resilience is real.

Marta finished her coffee and stood to leave. At the door, she turned back.

"Will anyone read this?" she asked.

I said I hoped so.

She nodded once, then walked out into the afternoon sun.

Acknowledgments

I've been conducting interviews with migrants since 2012—in Seattle, Los Angeles, Miami, along the border, and in communities throughout the country. I'm grateful to everyone who trusted me with their stories.

The University of Washington Center for Human Rights provided invaluable research on immigration enforcement. Their documentation of ICE operations and detention conditions informs several chapters of this book.

Taylor Hazan offered careful editing throughout the process.

I used AI tools to assist with drafting and revision. I reviewed and revised all text extensively, and I take full responsibility for its content.

Most of all, I thank the migrants themselves. This book exists because of your courage—in living these experiences, and in sharing them.